AWAKENING

JEREMY P.
TARCHER • PUTNAM
a member of
Penguin Putnam Inc.
New York

AWAKENING

A SUFI EXPERIENCE

Pir Vilayat
Inayat Khan

edited by Pythia Peay

Most Tarcher/Putnam books are available at special quantity
discounts for bulk purchases for sales promotions, premiums,
fund-raising, and educational needs. Special books or book
excerpts also can be created to fit specific needs.
For details, write Putnam Special Markets,
375 Hudson Street,
New York, NY 10014.

JEREMY P. TARCHER/PUTNAM
a member of
Penguin Putnam Inc.
375 Hudson Street
New York, NY 10014
www.penguinputnam.com

Library of Congress Cataloging-in-Publication Data

Inayat Khan, Pir Vilayat.
Awakening : a Sufi experience / Pir Vilayat Inayat Khan.
p.   cm.
ISBN 0-87477-974-X
1. Sufism.   I. Title.
BP189.I59   1999   99-17462   CIP
297.4'4—dc21

Printed in the United States of America
1   3   5   7   9   10   8   6   4   2

This book is printed on acid-free paper. ♾

BOOK DESIGN BY DEBORAH KERNER

CONTENTS

F O R E 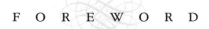 W O R D

To be at ease with God. To be like an infant in God's bosom. To be a child of the moment. To breathe well. These are some of the answers that the Sufis have given to the question "What does it mean to be a Sufi?"

Those who first adopted the name Sufi were devotees of the Prophet Muhammad's message of Unity who spurned the soul-numbing vanities of this world and the hereafter in the heat of their ardor for the intimacy of the Divine Presence. As these spiritual revolutionaries pooled their insights, a system of increasingly sophisticated contemplative techniques and metaphysical perspectives emerged under the tutelage of an expanding network of initiatic lineages.

One such lineage was the Chishti Order. With its creed of "Peace with All," its ecumenical outreach, and its taste for ecstatic music and dance, the Chishti Order has played a leading role in the spiritual life of India since it was first brought there by Khwaja Mu'inuddin Chishti more than seven hundred years ago.

From the shores of India, Sufism reached the West in the person of Hazrat Inayat Khan, the father of my father, Pir Vilayat. A highly distinguished musician and Pir (Sufi master) in the Chishti Order, Hazrat Inayat Khan traveled tirelessly in the United States and Europe in the 1910s and 1920s, performing the soulful classical music of India, preaching the message of "Love, Harmony, and Beauty," and initiating serious seekers in the mysteries of the inner life.

Hazrat Inayat Khan's work in the West expressed a deep commitment to ecumenism under the sign of the "Universal," the archetype of the spirituality of the future as he envisioned it, a Temple of Light in which all faiths converge in polyphonic glorification of the One Being. In this way he built on the advice of the great Andalusian Sufi master Ibn al 'Arabi (d. 1240), who wrote:

> Beware of confining yourself to a particular belief and denying all else, for much good would elude you—indeed, the knowledge of reality would elude you. Be in yourself a matter for all forms of belief, for God is too vast and tremen-

dous to be restricted to one belief rather than another.

Before returning to India, where he was to pass on from this world, Hazrat Inayat Khan designated his son, just ten years old at the time, as his successor. This summons has been the guiding force in Pir Vilayat's life. It inspired him, as a young man, to seek out the company of sages in the East and enter into long periods of seclusion and meditation. During these years he received training and confirmation as a Pir at the hands of Pir Fakhruddin, the son of his father's grandmaster.

Returning to Europe and North America, Pir Vilayat resumed his father's work, to which he has devoted himself with unflagging enthusiasm for the last four decades. As a child of both East and West, Pir Vilayat's unique contribution has been the reconciliation of the hallowed tradition of Sufism with the contemporary spirit of egalitarianism and advances in science and psychology. To this is added a serious concern for the social sphere, steeped in his own tragic experience of war and injustice as well as the liberating alchemy of Divinely inspired forgiveness.

Like his father before him, Pir Vilayat emphasizes experience over theory. His purpose is not to propagate doctrines so much as to beckon the awakening of the inner faculties possessed by each of us. This process of inner unveiling is ideally undertaken in the veiled environment of the spiritual retreat.

Indeed, the book you hold in your hands emerges from Pir Vilayat's work guiding spiritual seekers in the format of group retreats. Its chapters are compiled from transcriptions of his talks on these occasions. This was the invaluable contribution of Pythia Peay, a writer and longtime student of Sufism, who has pored over vast amounts of material to distill the ideas presented here. In editing and sometimes paraphrasing Pir Vilayat's words, she has succeeded wonderfully in unraveling the intricacies of his thought and expression to convey the broad sense of his teachings to the general reader, for whom the Sufi tradition tends to be terra incognita. Those who are approaching Pir Vilayat's teachings for the first time, or who have had difficulty comprehending his more esoteric Sufi writings, will no doubt find this book a gentle and forbearing companion.

Between the lines on the printed page lingers an experience of shared presence and deep attunement, an atmosphere suffused with the sacred. This original ambiance might be evoked by visualizing a scene such as this — an image of Pir Vilayat leading a morning meditation in a group retreat:

A regal old man sparkling with a vivacious serenity, cloaked in a burnoose as white as his beard, perches cross-legged on a rough wooden rostrum in a great canvas tent. The air is crisp as the sun rises up between snow-capped peaks. All around are seated men and women with closed eyes, a few half-asleep, but many rapt in a crystalline ecstasy, breathing light. His voice arises out of the silence, in a mild timbre that somewhat softens the edge of the challenge: "Dare you have the courage to be who you really are?"

— PIRZADE ZIA INAYAT KHAN

AWAKENING

ONE

AWAKENING
AND ILLUMINATION

"The fulfillment of this whole creation is to be found in man. And this object is only fulfilled when man has awakened that part of himself which represents the master, that is God himself."

— HAZRAT INAYAT KHAN

Imagine for a moment that you are a visitor from the far reaches of the Universe who has just landed on earth. If you revive the memory of the worlds you left behind, you will possess a rare knowledge that is not shared by most of the inhabitants of this small planet: a wide perspective and broad overview of the mystery of existence. In fact, you are a citizen of the Universe—not just the physical world, but all levels and spheres of reality. Perhaps you decided to come to earth because you wanted to experience its unique environment. Or, maybe your motivation was to make a mark, or to improve humankind's circumstances. In order to achieve these tasks, however, it was necessary to assume a body molded out of the fabric of your parents and ancestors; you chose them for the purposes of incarnation. As time passed, you became more adapted to your new physical and social environment—you worked hard, fell in love, developed friendships, started a family, and traveled the world. Gradually, the memory of your original home began to recede from consciousness, until finally it disappeared altogether.

For a while, your life on earth went smoothly; you were happy. Then you were affected by a major crisis, a personal upheaval, and life no longer seemed so certain. You began to feel restless and uneasy. The circumstances of your life felt frustrating, and you yearned for freedom. Stirred by nostalgia for something you couldn't even put a name to, you began looking up at the stars. Likewise, you started to feel an affinity with the trees, the butterflies, the sun, the animals, and the birds. In the vast reaches of the sky and the sweetness of nature, you rediscovered something of yourself that had been forgotten. Swept by feelings of awe and wonder, you began to have a dialogue within yourself about the nature of reality, and to question the source of all the beauty, suffering, and mystery of creation. Something incredible seemed to lie just behind the surface of things—yet the answer eluded you, slipping beyond the grasp of your realization.

Then suddenly, after years of searching, all the memories of your previous existence came back to you in a flash of awakening. Like the rediscovery of a precious relic hidden beneath layers of dirt, you rediscovered your true self, your real identity, which had been buried and forgotten in the depths of your unconscious. Once again, you could see through the vastly expanded perspective of this cosmic self, rather than the narrow vantage point of your earthly identity. It was as if the scales had fallen from your eyes; you possessed an x-ray-like intelligence that penetrated the truth concealed by the veil of creation—the revelation of the glory of the Universe—the One Being people call God. The miracle was that as you awakened, so, too, did the whole Universe. From the dance of the atoms and the choreography of the galaxies to the unfurling of a flower and the struggle for self-esteem in those who had been broken by life, the entire Cosmos resounded with the clarion call, "Awaken!" And though you found that you still had the same body, personality, relationships, and responsibilities as before, your experience of these circumstances had shifted dramatically: your awareness had become the lens through which God looked out upon the physical world; you had become "the eyes through which God sees." Your glance was the Divine glance.

In this parable is contained the essence of Sufism— the story of every soul's descent into existence, its experiences of suffering brought about by separation from its original state of being, and the subsequent journey of return and reawakening to its Divine nature. For from the moment the soul assumes a physical form, the memory of the celestial spheres from which it has descended is obscured; we remain conscious only of the things that have occurred to us since our birth. But the lost knowledge of the Universe still resides within our unconscious. Like an archaeologist who picks and tunnels through layers of stone, we can retrieve that knowledge by deepening and expanding our consciousness through meditation, prayer, and glorification. We get a feeling for what the state prior to our birth is like when we see the light in the eyes of a baby and think, as I often have: "I've seen this before. I remember that."

Indeed, the secret of Sufism is to shift from the vantage point of our personal point of view to the Divine point of view. Very simply, our being is made up of two poles of consciousness: the individual, personal self and the Divine, higher self. It is at the pole of the personal dimension of consciousness that we experience constraint and limitation. While we may think that our circumstances are the cause of this frustration, the real source lies in not being aware of our higher self. Thus, the goal in meditation is to reconnect our personal self to this transpersonal dimension of our being.

Another way to picture this process is to think of consciousness as if it were a pendulum. At one end is the dimension of our being that is transient and evanescent, or continually changing and transforming through a process of evolution. At the other end of this pendulum is that part of consciousness that remains immortal and unchanged. Thus our whole being could be said to be a continuity in change—just as it's never the same water that passes under the bridge, yet at the same time it's the same river. Each of these poles embodies a specific mode of consciousness.

Sufis make a distinction between acquired knowledge and revealed knowledge. Acquired knowledge is the information that we accumulate during the course of our everyday experience of life. But when we begin to view life through the antipodal standpoint—seeing through the eyes of God—then we access an inborn, intuitive, revealed knowledge that exists irrespective of the human condition. Meditation is the art of moving back and forth between two perspectives—the human and the Divine—downplaying one level in order to highlight the other. Eventually, we learn to extrapolate meaning from the synthesis of these different levels. This state is what I call awakening in life. For the culmination of the soul's journey of awakening is not just returning to its original state. Instead, it is how the soul has evolved through its passage on earth: what meaning has been extracted from its experiences; what archetypal qualities have unfolded as a result of the immense difficulties it has endured; and the unique way each soul's unfoldment has contributed to the evolution of the Universe itself.

Some may wonder what relevance such metaphysical truths have for the modern world—especially a world that appears to be moving farther away from the values of the ancient mystics and toward an increasingly impersonal, complex, and technological future. But it would seem that the times we live in underscore even more dramatically the need to distinguish between what has lasting value and what is only of passing worth; what takes the soul farther away from the Divine, and what brings it closer. The whole Cosmos moves as a pendulum: the past and the future, transiency and eternity, human and Divine. It is out of the ever-constant back-and-forth dialogue between these two poles that the future is created. I believe that the future is not just something waiting for us; it is something that is built by sorting through the past for that which belongs to tomorrow; it is a continual work-in-progress that takes place in every era and that occurs through each individual's innovative, imaginative, and conscious participation. It is what I call spiritual evolution.

As history proves, this process is one that stirs enormous resistance and difficulty. That the future is something we create, rather than passively endure, fills many with a sense of trepidation. To abandon the comfortable but worn-out values of the past feels like a free-fall into chaotic upheaval. But to fall back upon the comfort of the past, rather than move forward into the future, is to miss the rare cosmic opening that occurs in the flash of time between the past and the future in which it is possible to begin a new chapter in the evolving story of humankind. "The pull of the future," wrote

Leonhard Euler, "is stronger than the push of the past."
But what exactly is "the future"? According to the Sufi
worldview, the future means different things to different people. To some, the future is predetermined—a
fate fixed in stone that they must passively surrender to
in blind acquiescence. Others regard the future as
something that can be molded according to their individual will. From my perspective, the future appears to
be an outcome of both—and something much more.

The Sufis have developed a metaphysics of time and
fate dramatically different from the ordinary, linear
perception of time. For instance, they distinguish
between that moment when the past overlaps the
future in a way that inevitably shapes it, and a simultaneously occurring instant when the forward-moving
arrow of time is intersected by a transcendent dimension—like an infusion of fresh, uncreated energy into
circumstances that have become fixed and stagnant.
Using the physicist David Bohm's metaphor of the
ocean and the wave, this "time dynamic" could be
explained in the way that a wave of the sea rises, then
falls back into its oceanic depths; each new wave, however, is a fresh expression of the sea while interspersed
with elements of the previous wave.

Here we see the convergence of two forces: causality and the continually recurrent emergence of creative
new images and forms in the Universe—like the birth
of a star. It is not determined. For example, what
exactly do we mean by the concept of the "moment" or
"now"? If you are listening to music, the note you have

just heard continues to resound in your ears, even as you begin to take in the next note. In this "moment" there are no boundaries between the past or the future. Thus Sufis do not see individuals as victims of an inexorably preordained fate, nor as autocratic masters of their individual destiny. Rather, they take into account the existence of a higher intelligence that, through an innovative, trial-and-error, evolutionary process, is embedded within humanity to creatively shape and reshape life in an endless array of new images, patterns, and paradigms.

This transcendent force is what some call God and what I also call the "Universe," which may be the word which will be used at the millennium. Like a cosmic pull that exerts a force of its own over humanity, the Universe is constantly compelling us to break free of the conditioning of the past in order to transform and evolve. Just like the constant changes and adaptations in nature that have been occurring for aeons of time—resulting in emerald rain forests, exotic animals, and complex, intelligent creatures called people—this evolutionary force functions like a spiritual magnet to draw humanity beyond its limitations into further dimensions of consciousness and levels of perception. Indeed, the impetus to span the cleft from the past to the future is part of an ongoing, billions-of-years-old process by which the Universe has been fashioning its stardust into human beings. The planning of the Universe is affected by humankind's free, creative participation; thus the goal for humans is to become conscious of their profound impact upon the unfolding of creation. Should such a quantum shift in consciousness actually occur, it would represent an heroic victory over determinism—not over nature, but over the limitations of our own minds that prevent us from working in harmony with the Universe. Conscious evolution is humankind's final frontier, the ultimate freedom sought by humanity since the dawn of time. Thus the challenge seems to be one of overcoming the fear of the unexplored territory that lies ahead, and finding the courage and optimism to illuminate the spiritual dimension hidden within our nature. For it is the intuitive, radarlike quality of this transcendent faculty that will help to guide us through the darkness of the unknown—illuminating our minds and awakening our hearts to the splendor of a new consciousness.

"Participators in the evolution of the Universe": it is a phrase that resonates with possibility and potential. For this means to realize that the future is not just waiting to happen; instead, it is taking shape right here and now in the attitudes we hold, the choices we make, and the values we cherish. It means to become fully aware of the fact that humanity holds in its hands an extraordinary, precious opportunity to shape the future tomorrows of this planet. One way of doing this is through our Divinely inspired creativity—imagining and envisioning a world that is different from the one that has gone before. This does not mean abandoning all that humanity has attained thus far. Rather, it means carefully sifting through the past—preserving the legacy bequeathed by the great civilizations of antiquity, while at the same time improving our social structures to eschew the sad trail of suffering wreaked by the cruel against the victims of oppression.

The ongoing tension between the force of the past and the pull of the future can be seen in our time more clearly than ever. Evidence of a positive, forward-moving impulse toward the good, for example, is all around. Technologically, developments in communications are helping to bring the citizens of the planet into a more interdependent unity. Socially, new models of conflict resolution are being devised to help prevent violence, highlighting the importance of conscience in solving emotionally charged personal disputes. In the field of psychology, therapists are increasingly taking into account the spiritual concerns of their patients— the need for the sacred as a basis of self-esteem, as well as the recognition of an "immaculate child" at the core of the psyche undefiled by the surrounding environment. And in politics, forgiveness and reconciliation have introduced a new note into the fractiousness of rancorous debate, pouring a healing balm onto centuries-old wounds and offering the hope of peace.

Yet these advances are shadowed by a corresponding deterioration in moral values, as well as a stunted capacity for wisdom. These shortcomings are reflected in mounting social ills: an unprecedented population explosion amid the dwindling of the earth's precious natural resources, the frightening specter of vanishing landscapes and plant and animal species, ongoing religious and ethnic strife, and widespread poverty and violence. Thus even as part of humanity strives to dispel the darkness of human suffering through visionary paradigms and healing solutions, it is constantly being pulled back into the past by forces inimical to global spiritual ethics. The task at hand, it seems, is to find a way to bring those perceptions that are mired in petty narrowness and shortsightedness into alignment with the broader, more inclusive vision struggling to be born in our time.

THINKING
LIKE THE UNIVERSE

How is this awesome task to be accomplished? To the Sufis, the answer lies in the transformation of consciousness that occurs as the result of a shift in perspective from the personal point of view to the Divine point of view—what I call "thinking like the Universe." Plato illustrated man's ignorance by the allegory of the men chained in the cave who can see only shadows on the wall. In the same way, our everyday perspectives are illusory and therefore totally inadequate to making the quantum leap into a more evolved consciousness. We think, for instance, that it is the world that is our prison—whereas the prison is in our way of thinking and feeling. Caught in a vicious cycle of negativity that leads to despair, we give up any

hope of being able to fulfill our ideals. Buddha, however, saw that the only way to break free of the mental
chains that keep us bound in ignorance and misery is
by attaining freedom from the personal "I." The Sufis
say those commonplace thoughts and opinions blur our
innate connection to the Divine. Eventually, as we view
our problems through the eyes of the Universe, or God,
we come to realize that what we think is our problem
alone is the suffering of existence that is shared by
everyone. It is as if we have been participating in the
drama of the Universe—yet all we have been able to
think is "Why is this happening to me?" Indeed, if we
keep adding more and more people, *ad infinitum*, in
infinite regress, who share in the pain we think belongs
exclusively to ourselves, then we begin to glimpse the
reality behind the words of St. Francis of Assisi when
he said, "I thought I was looking at the world, but the
world is looking at me."

Like St. Francis, we cannot free ourselves from our
identification with our individual self unless we open
ourselves to the infinite dimension of the power of the
sacred. But the Universe is not just infinite, or sacred—
it is superlative; it is paramount. It is the very paragon
of what we mean by excellence. As it has been described
by mystics since the beginning of time, to glimpse the
true nature of the Universe is like awakening from a
clouded trance. "Imagine," says Hazrat Inayat Khan,
"that you're awake and walking about amongst people
who sleep; how can you communicate with them? You
realize that they can have no idea about your awareness

because they're still sleeping. You used to be like that yourself. But now you are awake." This is what Christ meant when he said, "They know not what they do."

I remember, for example, sitting in an ice cream parlor with my two little boys. I had just come out of a retreat and was feeling high because of my meditations. Then I thought to myself, "If only the people around me knew what they're missing." In another example, I recall making a visit to a *rishi* who was in seclusion in a cave high up in the Himalayas. I was traveling with a group of people as it was a very dangerous jungle with lots of wild animals. One of the members of the group asked the *rishi* something that, to me, was very mundane. Fascinated, I watched the *rishi* struggle to come down from his state of Divine ecstasy and enter into the mind of that person in order to answer his question.

But witnessing the phenomenon of life from a transcendental overview doesn't serve just to lift one up out of the trenches of existence. In the original Indian custom, people may leave the world to become ascetics. If that thinking is imported to the West without showing what light it can throw on people's problems, it can make people otherworldly. Broadening our attunement beyond the horizons of the individual self, however, awakens one to the meaning encoded into existence— a kind of cognitive "super-logic" that reveals a different purpose, a larger pattern, than anything we might previously have imagined. There is a story about Albert Einstein that illustrates this. It was said that he was pushing his baby in a pram in the midst of downtown New York City. As he was engaged in this seemingly mundane task, he was envisioning the planet whirling within the solar system, and the solar system whirling within the Milky Way—and so on throughout the Cosmos. Even in the crowded hustle and bustle of everyday life, Einstein's perspective allowed him to see himself within the context of the totality of this marvelous creation.

And that is exactly what spiritual awakening is— shifting from one perspective to another, until we finally glimpse meaningfulness where our mind could not perceive it before. The higher and broader the perspective, the more inclusive it is. The pictures we see in holograms extrapolate different vantage points because they involve the whole hologram rather than just a slice of it. When we look at our problems, for instance, we can see that there are different levels of meaning in our problems. We think we grasp what is being enacted in the problem; then we see that there is another level from which it looks entirely different— instantaneously something becomes clear to us, and we didn't do anything! It's totally impromptu, unexpected. We really have the feeling, "This was revealed to me." In this moment of revelation, it is as if the light of intelligence has enhanced the very aura surrounding our bodies. Just as when we grasp something that we've never understood before—suddenly there is a smile, an outburst of energy, and a breakthrough of light. One's whole being burns with a brighter flame because of the intensity of awareness—as if the luminosity of our awareness has sparked the very cells of our body. Indeed, awakening triggers off illumination; it is always connected to light. But it isn't an intellectual process; it has to do with the radiance of luminous thoughts—a kind of clarity that overcomes ambiguity because light highlights things and makes everything clear.

There is an adage pertaining to this process of awakening and illumination. Newton said, "I think as God thinks." Scientists in those days were shocked by what he was saying. But what he meant was that if a physicist has a sense of the intention behind the workings of the Universe, it's because his mind thinks as the universe thinks, only less well—just as the fraction of a hologram behaves less well than the whole hologram, but still behaves like the hologram. In the same way, individuals who intuit the Divine intention behind their problems do so because they have recognized that their thinking is isomorphic with—or the "same as"—the thinking of the Universe. Their thinking is cosmic; they have reconnected to the totality in the same way one would recharge a battery by plugging it into an electrical source. The consequence of linking one's thinking and awareness with the thinking and awareness of the Universe is that it brings about a dramatic change in how we see life—jumpstarting individuals out of the limitations of their narrow thinking patterns that continue round and round in the usual deep ruts.

Even more significantly, this kind of personal

awakening is not isolated in its effects. As the physicist David Bohm writes, a deep change in meaning is a catalyst for transformation "in the deep structure of the brain. The new meaning will produce different thoughts, and therefore an entirely different function of the brain. . . . As this changes, the whole universe changes." As individuals alter their consciousness, so, too, do they effect a transformation in the surrounding environment. This represents a breathtaking breakthrough that radically distinguishes the spirituality of the future from that of the past. The Universe is evolving toward an even greater destiny—and we are the means of this global transformation! This means that instead of assuming that the blueprint for the future has already been designed, we realize that the future is being constructed step-by-step through an innovative trial-and-error process—imaged and designed through our participation in the Divine Programming.

Portents of this emerging spiritual process can already be seen. Many religious denominations, for instance, are being impacted by a growing weariness regarding the "institutionalization" of faith in its varied forms—and by the need to make a clear distinction between spirituality and religion. The need for believers of many faiths who feel strongly compelled to free themselves from outdated belief systems such as dogma, superstition, customs, prescriptions, and hackneyed concepts is growing increasingly stronger. Here, doubt is not an enemy of faith, but a servant that can help liberate individuals from the constraints of narrow conditioning, replacing theoretical belief with direct mystical experience. The concept of God, says Hazrat Inayat Khan, is the first step, the second step is the experience of God, and the third is awakening to the God within.

A second hallmark of the spirituality of the future is a recognition of the need for seekers to trust their conscience and assume responsibility for their own development rather than relying on role models to dictate prescriptive "do's and don'ts." This leads naturally to the third portent of the new spirituality—a transformation in how we envision the Divine. For while in the past individuals may have posited a "perfect God" who wreaks upon humankind a harshly preordained fate, a radically different image of the Divine is appearing on the horizon: the Universe as a Global Being of which the Cosmos is a body, whose intelligence flashes through our thoughts and emotions, sparking ecstasy and despair in the cosmic drama—and in which we participate by our individual free will.

We need to take into account the reverse and recognize the effects of the thinking of the Universe upon our thinking, the intention of the Universe upon our planning, and the emotions of the Cosmic Drama upon our value systems. From this perspective, the Universe is an impersonal virtuality—a limitless potentiality—that is not static but continually evolving through "you" and "me." Revisioning God as the Universe has staggering implications for how we view reality.

Clearly, apprehending the effects of this transpersonal dimension upon our everyday lives cannot be grasped through the deductive reasoning and ordinary logic people so commonly rely upon to solve their problems. Though useful for coping with tasks like buying stocks or running a business, these mental perspectives are too narrow a lens through which to see the magnitude of the creative programming of the Universe at work in our lives. Instead, we need to explore a transcendent logic that could help us perceive the intricate, interconnective elements underlying seemingly unrelated external causes—what the Swiss psychologist Carl Jung called synchronicity, and others call miracles, strange coincidence, or the hand of fate. Training ourselves to see through the eyes of God, as the Sufis say, has enormous potential to heal psychological wounds and spiritual emptiness. This enhanced insight grasps patterns and meaningful connections where there may have been only a disconcerting sense of randomness and isolation—a clockwork universe. Indeed, awakening to the meaningfulness of life is a potent medicine for modern ills, sparking a leap from amazing meaningfulness to ever greater patterns of purposefulness and intention.

But exactly how does one go about "thinking like the Universe," or "seeing through the eyes of God," broadening our vision to perceive the patterns underlying our lives? It is not so simple a matter as changing the nature of our thoughts through reading, reciting affirmations, or attending lectures or conferences, though that is a step forward. Instead, the mind of the Universe is accessed through meditative, non-ordinary states of consciousness—those wordlessly profound transpersonal dimensions described by the great mystics. It is our encounter with this "other reality" that catalyzes a dramatic shift in perspective, widening the lens of our individual psyches and revealing the immense scope of the Divine point of view. Such expanded states of consciousness are not illusory, as some critics claim, but are reflected in the theories of scientists at the leading edge of physics. In meditation, for instance, we may experience an altered notion of space—being both everywhere and in one place—that corresponds to quantum theories of non-locality in space. Time, as well, may shift from being linear and one-dimensional to a multi-tiered dimension influenced by what scientists describe as acausal and nondetermined factors.

From these dramatic shifts in vantage point of space and time, it is possible to glimpse clues into the workings of the Cosmos. For according to the ancient teachings of the Sufis, we are not separate from this transcendent reality. Rather, they taught that we are a continuum of consciousness ranging from the boundless, transpersonal dimension that is coextensive with all others to the "discrete entity" that makes up our unique individuality. Learning to embrace these two ends of the continuum is the spiritual task of awakening and illumination—reconciling the seemingly irreconcilable vantage points between the Divine and individual points of view. In contradistinction to the

Hindu yogic perspective, however, in this state of awakening in Sufism one does not need to give up one's personal identity, but instead learn how to correlate it with one's Divine dimension. Furthermore, Sufis train their consciousness to shift back and forth between the Divine and human vantage points; the infinite and the finite; and the archetype and the exemplar.

To explain the dynamic interplay that takes place along the axis of self and Divine, Sufis often rely on the concept of an archetype. Contrast, for instance, the concept of "roundness" with an actual round table, or the idea of "rosehood" with roses growing in a garden. Like Jungians, Sufis posit a realm of archetypes, or transcendental patterns, that shape material reality. Thus "rosehood" would correspond to the Divine mode of thinking, while the actual red, yellow, or white rose would be a unique expression, or exemplar, of that archetype in material reality.

Contemplating the Universe in its boundless spectrum of archetypes is the basis of the Sufi practice of invoking the names of God. Glorifying and exulting God's attributes through our prayers and concentrations arouses those very qualities in ourselves—in other words our attunement shapes our being. Meditating on the clarity of Divine intelligence, for instance, sparks the light of the aura, while emotionally attuning to Divine majesty or sublime beauty shapes the etheric field of the body along the lines of those archetypal templates. According to their attunement, one person may radiate wisdom, another a commanding presence of authority, and yet another a refined spirit of loveliness. Thus in meditation we not only discover the reality of the Universe behind all existence but also as it is reflected in ourselves. Discovering the Universe manifested within us allows us to accept the beauty of our being as we never could have done before, releasing potentialities which would have remained latent. We could not have achieved this if we had tried to mold ourselves through our individual will.

In turn, manifesting the Divine Qualities in everyday existence has a transforming effect upon the Universe itself. One of Ibn 'Arabi's tenets is that in our prayers, God recurrently creates and re-creates Himself: *"al-Haqq al-Makhluq fi'l-l'tiqadat"* (the God created in the beliefs). In contemporary terminology, we could imagine the Universe as seeking to discover itself through us. Ibn 'Arabi advances the picture of God discovering Himself through a mirror. To quote the Qur'an "Wheresoever you turn, there is the face of God" (2, 115); and, "The sights do not reach Him, He reaches the sights" (6:103); and, in the *Hadith* (sayings of the Prophet Muhammad), "God created Adam in His own form." The ancient dervishes as well envisioned the Universe as seeking to discover itself through us by actuating its qualities in the expression of our personalities and even in our countenance. Imagine: the intelligence and ecstasy of the Universe awakening in our awareness, transfiguring the very contours of our physical being! Generalizing from this, it follows that conscious awareness has a transforming effect upon the Universe, and vice versa. Says Ibn 'Arabi of this circular, mystical exchange, "He is at the same time the One who reveals Himself (*motajali*) and that through which He manifests Himself." So God discovers Himself by revealing Himself to you in the form through which He projects His attributes as your unique physical countenance. "Wheresoever you turn, there is the face of God" (Qur'an 2:115). God's actuality is a virtuality that becomes a reality as ourselves. Sufism is very challenging. Ibn 'Arabi reverses all the old notions of God "up there" and us down here as "miserable worms" (to borrow from Pascal). Thus, Sufis see God as being awakened not just in us, but as us.

This kind of creative interplay between human and Divine has exciting implications for how we currently envision spiritual unfoldment. Rather than seeing the Universe as a remote, unchanging paradise that is separate from the illusory existence of the created world— something to be attained by overcoming the lures and distractions of the material world—in the language of the future we might say instead that the Universe is discovering and re-creating itself as it evolves through the course of our human lives. Thus our conscious participation in creating the future could be seen as an extension of the self-organizing activity of the Universe—in other words, the Universe itself is the transcendent power motivating our higher aspirations and noble ideals of peace, harmony, beauty, and truth. Each of us has felt this in the most intimate way: in a powerful longing to be of service in building a better world; in the nostalgia to experience sublime emotions such as compassion, majesty, or splendor; or even in the desire to understand the Divine intent behind the personal suffering each person endures in life—and to relieve pain with compassion and mercy.

Such a way of thinking, however, raises some provocative metaphysical questions. Is the Universe as a global reality self-aware? Does a global consciousness lie behind our individual consciousness? Does the Universe itself "think"? Conversely, does our expanding realization of the Universe contribute to the knowledge that the Universe has of itself? Does it, in fact, advance that knowledge? And, most important, does that enhanced intelligence play a role in determining the fate of humanity as it struggles to overcome the cosmic dramas of suffering, ignorance, poverty, and violence being enacted on a global scale?

Such questions are not merely the abstract thoughts of spiritual seekers isolated from the joys and sadnesses of everyday life. Sufism emphasizes in its teachings that in order to evolve rather than simply continue on in the same way century after century, humanity needs to enlist the pull of an "attractor"—another dimension irrespective of location in space. This attractor lies outside what the Buddhists call the *samsaric* "wheel of becoming." For though the future is not yet here, we build it by being pulled toward a horizon that recedes continually, Point Omega. This can happen only if each of us lets go of the way we are in our "skinbound" identity and imagines instead how we could be if we manifested even a fraction of the richness of the Universe—making the "possible potential" a reality on earth.

The Sufis poetically describe this evolutionary spiritual process as manifesting the "Divine inheritance." For example, if a peaceful person comes into the room, someone might say, "It's wonderful to see a peaceful person." The dervish, however, would say instead, "Isn't it wonderful to see Divine peace coming through this person?" What they mean by this is that the human personality has the potential to become the vehicle of the Universe's archetypes. This is the intention behind the practice of *wazaif* (repetition of sacred phrases, or names of God, representing various Divine attributes): to connect a specific quality in oneself to its source in the Universe (God). The Qur'an states, for instance, that there is nothing on earth that does not have its correspondence at the super-celestial level, or the "Divine Treasury." Thus you might imagine a ladder that allows you to ascend to the place from where such qualities descend into your character. The metaphor of the ladder illustrates that attributes such as courage or dignity do not have their source in the individual ego, but are cosmic in origin.

The idea that the celestial realm of archetypes can be brought into reality through the personality of the individual adds a sense of purposefulness to the practice of meditation, deepening it into an activity that is of service to humanity. Every time you confront a specific challenge or problem in life by contemplating what it is that the Universe is asking from you in response—

whether it is cultivating the quality of forgiveness, for example, or wisdom, truth, or courage—it is as if you have declared your wish to be of service to the Universe by actuating one of its Divine Qualities in your being. This establishes a connection between the two levels, or poles of being—the Divine and the personal. According to a noble Sufi tradition, this connection between God and man is like the medieval covenant of fealty that once existed between a king and the knight who served him. Rather than an earthly kingdom, however, this sacred covenant reflects a pledge each soul made in pre-eternity before incarnation to affirm and serve the Divine Sovereignty while on earth. Indeed, attuning to the thinking of the Universe through meditation is like becoming privy to the secrets of the king. Meditators become like "ambassadors of the Universe," whose mission is to display the qualities of the Divine King or Queen to whom they have dedicated their lives in eternal service. Their personalities robed in the richness of the Being of the Universe, they display their royal attributes in the same way ambassadors display medals, ribbons, and uniforms.

SHIFTING BETWEEN THE HUMAN AND DIVINE PERSPECTIVES

∞

All ambassadors undergo a rigorous training before becoming diplomats of the royal court. Likewise, spiritual seekers who seek to become "transparent to the Divine" must first become skilled at learning how to "think like the Universe." For just as the job of a diplomat is to deliver messages from the sovereign to foreign countries, the task of individuals-of-conscience is to impart the wisdom of the Divine intelligence. Training oneself to see things from the Divine point of view is key to understanding the essence of Sufism: it is the "global compass" that offsets the personal vantage point, the "true north" orienting one's direction in life. This is why the Sufis aim at downplaying their personal view in order to espy the Divine point of view.

Meditation and contemplation are the training grounds for this practice. Here, we become adept at learning to shift our consciousness from one perspective to another—moving between individual consciousness and cosmic consciousness, somewhat like the graduation of perspectives contained within a hologram. For example, you could think of the Universe out there as "other" and separate. Or, conversely, you could imagine that the starry Cosmos has converged itself as your body and is looking at itself through your eyes. Experimenting with changes in our mode of thinking is what leads to the state of awakening called illumination by the mystics, just as discovering the cosmic and transcendent dimensions of our being broadens and transforms our formerly constricted understanding of life.

One can begin working with altered states of consciousness by stepping back and observing how we ordinarily "see" what goes on around us. Imagine, for a moment, that you are training your sight upon a deeper reality that is transpiring behind the moving scene of everyday life. You may be watching a rustic country scene, scanning the starry sky, or enjoying a glorious sunrise. You may be sipping coffee in a sidewalk café on the Champs Élysées in Paris, observing life as it passes by: honking cars, men and women, young and old, intent on their business or casually dawdling. You may be watching a fight on Fourteenth Street in New York City, observing a mugging in London, participating in political demonstrations in Italy, being moved by the wonder of a baby being born, or being saddened by a loved one dying.

Behind this shifting panorama we may gradually begin to sense the larger emotions of the human drama: pain, cruelty, injustice, greed, terror, heroism, love, disenchantment. From yet another perspective, people seem inescapably conditioned, caught in the cogs of the wheels of a gigantic social power system which we call civilization. Or, if we tilt consciousness yet another way, the mass of humanity appears as ripples in an ever-recurring flow of ongoing life. By shifting perspectives the way a child turns a kaleidoscope, we gradually see that all these perspectives are merely the veils over a concealed dimension of reality lying just beyond ordinary cognition. "Knowledge," writes Ibn 'Arabi, "is a veil upon the known."

In fact, according to the Qur'an, all that we perceive externally in the world of existence are signs, *ayat*—

clues to the intention and meaningfulness lying just behind and beneath the surface of life. The scientist Heinz Pagels says, "I think the Universe is a message written in a cosmic code, and the scientist's job is to decipher that code." While scientists observe electrons and manipulate matter to decode the riddle of creation, spiritual adepts study consciousness and cognitive realities to uncover the true nature of reality. The mystical yearning to understand existence is often triggered by a sensation of feeling suffocated. Life feels like a hoax; one becomes driven to see what's behind it. One's task becomes to grasp the meaningfulness underlying the programming of the Cosmos, without being biased by the physical world whereby it initially reveals itself—a difficult undertaking!

How does one go about gaining insight into the deepest levels of reality? First, by dropping the biases of ordinary thinking that obscure the interconnection with the Universe. Bistami, a dervish who lived in the mountains for forty years, said, "God fools you in the markets of this world. Now when you see His effigies, they are just devices. The reality is hidden behind them." He goes on to say, "The bridegroom doesn't have to suffice himself with the veil of the bride." Stripped of the veil of the illusory, ephemeral traces of everyday experience, our minds may gradually, in infinite regress, begin to perceive remote glimmers of the thinking of the Universe. Ultimately, we may reach a stage in our meditations where we discover a direct intuition of meaningfulness unmediated by physical phenomena. Hazrat Inayat Khan says that when intelligence is confronted with an object it becomes consciousness, and when it is voided of any content it returns to its ground, which is intelligence.

Attainment of this "spiritual intelligence" is the ultimate realization of mystics. Sufis call this state of consciousness *Jabarut*, the ground out of which consciousness emerges. For as ordinary consciousness is gradually freed from the perspectives of everyday existence—thoughts, ideas, circumstances, emotions, physical events—the transcendent dimension begins to emerge. What do we mean by transcendence? Take, for example, an apple tree in blossom. Though your glance takes in its trunk, branches, leaves, and flowers, you are also moved by its beauty and loveliness. And while the beauty of this tree depends upon its physical form, still, it has an essential reality of its own which is its meaningfulness. Or, take music: behind the notes are an array of vibrational frequencies that could be said to constitute the language of the thinking of the Universe. Likewise, it is the meaning—not the letters—that shine through the words of a book or text. So the mind, stripped of the distraction of transient thoughts, is infused with an inborn sense of meaningfulness. This transcendent faculty appears only when one has given up trying to sort things out in an habitual fashion.

Once while on retreat in the Alps, I had just such a breakthrough experience—one that was dramatically reflected in the weather and surrounding landscape. After a stormy night in the mountains, precariously sheltered beneath the roof of a shepherd's shed, I observed the dark clouds and heard the thunderclaps gradually receding into the distance, swept away by a raging wind. As if in sympathetic resonance, my consciousness began to melt away, scattering into an infinite, edgeless Universe. Vanishing along with the storm were my concepts about the world, the Cosmos, my personal circumstances, unresolved problems, values, appropriate or inappropriate actions—even my teachings about the Divine Qualities, the meaningfulness of life, egos, bodiness, the psyche. Suddenly, all these thoughts seemed so futile, worthless, and misleading!

Rather than flounder in a "dark night" of negativity brought on by the collapse of these mental structures, however, I clung to the very meaningfulness that had just shattered my commonplace thinking. It was the consummate quantum leap; it brought vividly alive the last words spoken by my father, Hazrat Inayat Khan, on his deathbed: "When the unreality of life strikes my heart, its reality is revealed to me." All my life, I thought to myself, I have prided myself on what I thought were valid theories about the Universe—unmasking the hoax of superstitions, dogmas, and conditioned responses to life. But instead of dismissing all these constructs, I realized that they had acted as stepping-stones that led me to this ultimate breakthrough. Even though I now had no more use for them, they remained there for my use, like a ladder propped against a wall, while "I" became immersed in the sublime, wordless state of unity beyond life—existence unveiled into eternity.

How to explain the unutterable beauty of this mystery? We seek knowledge and understanding, for instance—but do we know the Knower? We have been listening to music—but do we know the Composer? Music, for instance, is a reflection of the composer's being, just as the Cosmos is an expression of the Universe. But in the same way that it is impossible to grasp the entire scope and range of the composer through his or her compositions, so the physical manifestations of the Universe are but a fragment of the Being whose totality eludes our grasp. Can you, however, imagine what it would be like to listen to a piece of music as it originally formed within the composer's mind, note upon note arising into consciousness, arranging themselves into a symphony or a song? Such an experience would yield a totally different insight into his nature. Rather than seeing the composer as a body, mind, personality, or psyche, from this illumined perspective we would see him as the repository of original intention. This is exactly the shift in consciousness during meditation whereby we experience what it is to "think like the Universe." In our ordinary experience, for instance, we think in terms of duality: we know another and even represent the "known" as "other" than oneself. But here at the summit, all is one. "Where there is duality," it says in the Brihad Aranyaka Upanishad, "whereby can the known know Himself?"

For the Sufis, one can be liberated from the prison

of duality to attain the liberty of at-onement only through the magical spell of unconditional love—that ecstatic embrace that bridges the separation between lover and beloved. In words resonant with yearning, Sufi poets such as Rumi have described how the human lover makes the Divine Beloved into the "worshiped One," or *ma'abud*. According to Ibn 'Arabi, God is the One whom every lover loves in every beloved. In turn, the force of love emanated by the Divine Lover toward the human being makes of that person the "loved one," or *mahboob*. Thus through the reciprocal glorification between love, lover, and Beloved in the realm of the sacred, there is no separation between "I" and "Thou," but a union of two into one. As the Sufi mystic al Hallaj expressed it, "I am He whom I love; and He whom I love is I. We are two spirits dwelling in one body. If thou seest me, thou seest Him, and if thou seest Him, thou seest us both." This stage, says Hazrat Inayat Khan, is "just like touching the presence of God," which is that part of oneself that is not subject to death.

Like the inevitable swing of the pendulum, however, consciousness cannot remain in sublime transcendence—or *samadhi*—but must naturally swing back from this pinnacle of realization into the individual, personal perspective. But, like the traveler who returns from foreign lands laden with precious jewels and priceless treasures, the seeker does not return to ordinary consciousness unchanged or empty-handed, but emanating the exotic perfume of his or her spiritual realization. The experience of this deathless state beyond life is, like the legendary philosopher's stone, the mystical magic that infuses ordinary existence with "the life of life"—a meaningfulness beyond meaning emanating from beyond the framework of space and time. Buddha describes this as the "non-become." A timeless energy, it yet impacts the process of becoming and unfolding in life. Like the lightning *vajra* of the Tibetans that strikes unexpectedly and overwhelmingly, the flare of insight triggers off a revolutionary leap in consciousness, catalyzing dormant potentialities into realities. For to awaken in life, we first must awaken beyond life. As the radiation of the sun powers the unfurling of the seed into a plant, so, too, does the light of spiritual realization alter modes of thinking, dramatically restructuring the formation of the ego. As much as one might wish to change one's individual personality, it can only truly be transformed under the impact of illuminated insights into the meaningfulness of life. Then, one can begin to see one's circumstances in the light of the Divine Being—one's individual intention is corrolated with the Divine Intention, one's personal understanding is illuminated with Divine Understanding, and one's personal love is suffused with Divine Love.

∞

In the following chapters, each of the themes I have mentioned so far will be taken up and explored in greater depth and detail, along with accompanying guided meditations, the repetition of names of God, and breathing practices. The book is arranged in such a way that it follows a pattern repeatedly emphasized in all my teachings: the journey of awakening *beyond* life—or experiencing a spectrum of altered states of consciousness—is followed by that of awakening *in* life, or applying these states of consciousness to one's personal circumstances. This twofold process mirrors the classic retreat in which the seeker turns away from the demands of the world in order to undergo an alchemical process of transmutation, then returns to the world renewed and with a radically altered perspective.

Thus, chapter 2 begins with the first stage in the retreat process, in which a person withdraws from the demands of the world in order to open to the finer dimensions of the inner world. Chapter 3 further expands ordinary consciousness through an exploration of the various states of consciousness and perspectives embodied by the world's great masters, saints, and prophets. This is followed by chapter 4, in which the meditator ventures far beyond the realms of everyday consciousness into the landscapes of light, the realms of the celestial angels and archangels, and transcendent states of unity.

Chapter 5 begins the path back into the world through a meditation on the Divine Treasury of archetypal qualities, and how they not only help us solve the difficulties and problems we face in everyday life but are the fruit of our struggles as well. Chapter 6 outlines two ancient Sufi practices, whirling and the *dhikr*, that further deepen the process of awakening in life by creating a temple for the Divine Presence on earth out of the fabric of the body. Finally, chapter 7 calls upon us to create heaven on earth through the awakening of the Divine Conscience—or the way in which our personal values can help midwife into existence a spiritual value system that will ensure a more conscious, compassionate, and beautiful future for all humankind.

TWO

BEGINNING
THE JOURNEY:

According to Sufi tradition, in his training, the Pir has to undergo a forty-day retreat of fasting and constant repetition of sacred phrases from morning to evening.

A mystical process that is valued by many traditions, the retreat experience embodies an important spiritual principle: one cannot begin to perceive the subtle levels of reality without first quieting the grosser vibrations of the outside world. Everyday reality is so striking that one has to make a conscious effort to downplay it in order to see the other reality that lies behind it. It is common for meditators to adopt a physical position of stillness in a quiet space set aside from the whir and bustle of everyday life. Shielded against the intrusions of the environment, one is isolated from disturbing events such as economic crises, wars, and terrorist bombings, as well as from one's own personal emotional reactions. In effect, a meditation retreat— whether one hour, one day, or forty days—allows the seeker a way to loosen the ties of his worldly responsibilities in order to turn within.

"Loosen the ties" is a phrase from my father, Hazrat Inayat Khan; he doesn't say to cut the ties completely, for if you do that then you become an ascetic—you might as well go and live in the Himalayas. So that's not the answer. The story of the Gordian knot helps to explain the danger that lies in cutting ties completely. As the tale goes, there was a knot in a city in Anatolia—whoever could untie that knot, it was said, would end up conquering the world. Alexander the Great decided to make a try; failing to loosen it, he lost patience and severed the cords, thereby losing his chance to conquer the world. The message implicit in this myth is that the only way to loosen the ties that bind us is by finding freedom within—freedom not from circumstances, but from our conditioned thoughts and emotions.

Indeed, in stark contrast to the ancient world, where humans were but a fragile presence against the backdrop of a vast expanse of wilderness, the need for solitude is never more urgent than in today's teeming, techno-industrial world. One's identity is easily lost in all the agitation, grossness, violence, dishonesty, selfishness, and greed so common to urban society. The busy person who must shoulder tremendous responsibilities while keeping track of a myriad of details is by now a familiar cliché. It's true that one has to be very capable and organized in today's world—or else risk homelessness and poverty. Yet on the other hand, if that is the only purpose in life, one is driven to ask the question "Is this all there is?" One lives in a state that fosters competition and envy. Frustration and hopelessness can set in: "I'm not getting anywhere in my life. What's it all about? I'm no good."

Gripped by despair or meaninglessness, it is no wonder that so many people today are filled with a yearning to reconnect to a deeper sense of self. And while a busy professional may be one model of success, the way of life offered by those mystics who spend their days wholly absorbed in the Divine Presence offers contemporary humanity a different kind of attunement— one that could permeate our day-to-day lives, throw light on our problems, and help unfurl the potentials of our being. Imagine, for instance, visiting Mount Athos in Greece, where there are monks who spend their days and nights in prayer, and the powerful blessing and mood of sacredness manifests through their beings. If you have ever listened to a recording of Orthodox chants, you can hear how a serene, heavenly music comes through their voices—the music of the celestial spheres. These monastics may be unadapted to life as we know it. But they fulfill an important function in the world by reminding us of a dimension of existence that is quashed by our frenetic activities and desire for power, pleasure, and possessions.

Not everyone is called to become a monk or a nun.

And many people approach meditation as a means to relieve stress rather than enter into a communion with God. But stress reduction is not illumination; in fact, that approach, while helpful in lowering blood pressure, rarely leads to genuine enlightenment. Rather, the crux of spiritual work is the deep transformation and expansion of consciousness that occurs through awakening. Meditation, in fact, could be defined as the art of modulating consciousness. Like musicians who deepen their talent through hours of practicing scales, meditators' creative discipline involves mastering a range of cognitive perceptions. A retreat provides a venue within which seekers can explore the landscapes of the spiritual universe—the dimensions of consciousness that lie within. Experienced meditators, for instance, observe that as they alter their field of consciousness, notions of space, time, light, sound, identity, and causality vary across a wide spectrum that ultimately gives rise to different modes of thinking, or ways of perception. Indeed, in Sufi meditations, we clearly distinguish between four modes of thinking that correspond to four states of consciousness that exist beyond the ordinary middle range.

Like a pebble thrown into a placid pool of water that creates ever-widening circles, for instance, it is common during meditation for consciousness to expand, encompassing increasingly wider fields of awareness. As this happens, so, too, does our notion of our physical "self" expand, becoming more cosmic and less individualized. We have a sense that our bodies are surrounded by zones of subtle matter, like a magnetic field. Such an experience dissolves our skinbound organism into a subtle electromagnetic field radiantly extending into space. This gives rise to an experience of being physically dispersed throughout the entire creation, as if our bodies were bits of the rapidly expanding stardust that came into existence a thousandth of a second after the Big Bang.

A second mode of consciousness involves a shift away from the all-embracing cosmic consciousness to the space within. From this interior vantage point, the external structures of the world reveal themselves as reflections of what the physicist David Bohm describes as the "implicate" order—the fundamental reality behind our perception of the physical world. This reflects the traditional Islamic view that the external objects of material reality are but the traces of a deeper reality, and a clue toward grasping it. Says Ibn 'Arabi, Sufis seek to grasp "that which transpires through that which appears." By viewing reality as something that moves from the inside to the outside—as if emerging out of mysterious, unsounded depths—our minds grasp interconnectedness, perceiving patterns of meaningfulness not seen in waking consciousness.

In yet a third setting of consciousness, we shift from the interior depths to the peaks of transcendence. I recall moments, like the scent of a flower that lingers, from my own retreats in India—meditating at the source of the Ganges in the cool of dawn, while surrounded by *sannyasins* immersed in a state of timeless tranquillity.

Physical reality appears far off, as if I were an eagle flying over the earth's terrain. From this transcendent perspective, the very notion of space itself disappears as
consciousness becomes absorbed into infinity. Though
it is difficult to explain the transcendent faculty of our
minds, the mathematician Henri Poincaré defined
infinity as the ability of the mind to image a number
greater than the greatest number envisioned so far in
infinite regress. As opposed to the personal pole of our
identity, this is the impersonal, transcendent pole of our
self, that part of us that has awakened beyond life. Thus
eschewing the notion of physical substantiality, our
sense of identity shifts from bodiness to pure intelligence. This mode of perception permits one to grasp the
essence behind the fabric of life.

Finally, there is a setting of consciousness that
incorporates all previous modes of thinking. This is a
state that embraces both the knowledge acquired from
one's personal experience of life and the transcendent
intelligence independent of external conditions. One
attains an overview of all types of cognitive perception.
The Swiss psychiatrist C. G. Jung spent much time
pondering the mysterious relationship between the
psyche and the physical world. He discovered that in
some cases the psyche influences the events in our lives,
rather than merely being impacted by external events.
The spiritual contemplative could extrapolate from
this notion of synchronicity the idea that the mental
and material realities are like two sides of the same
coin—so interconnected that body involves mindness

and vice versa. Body/mind connectivity supports the view that our meditative experiences of awakening and illumination influence both the unseen dimension of the invisible world and our surrounding physical environment. Ultimately, we arrive at the realization that what affects one area of the "psycho-eco-system" affects every other area.

Once meditators become adept at modulating consciousness in all its perspectives, they enjoy the benefits of an evolved intelligence that sparks their innovative faculties. This expanded awareness allows them to gain insight into the solutions of personal problems that appeared so stubbornly elusive from the vantage point of the personal ego. Thus meditation is the wellspring of creativity, leading to works of art, a more beautiful personality, more harmonious relationships—even insight into intractable social problems such as environmental pollution or war. In other words, a change in consciousness effects a change in our circumstances as well.

Thus I want to reiterate that the process I am elaborating here and throughout this book is a twofold one: awakening beyond life must occur before we can awaken in life—I am convinced that that is the only way. What this means is that one sometimes has to call a halt to daily life, either through a disciplined regimen of daily meditations or, if possible, by going on a retreat. It's as if we must take a break from the demands of everyday life in order to awaken a part of ourselves that has been asleep. Then, when we return to life, the task is to try to remain awake. For when a person re-enters life after a period of meditation or a long retreat, that person has gained a certain protection against the onslaught of circumstances and is able to maintain a transcendent overview even in the middle of the gravity pull that drags people back down into commonplace ways of thinking. The best image I have for the state of conciousness I am trying to convey is of Baha'u'llah (the founder of the Baha'i faith) sitting in a smelly, sordid prison without toilets while maintaining a very high attunement, thereby demonstrating that a mystic can be spiritually awake even in the midst of the worst suffering and tragedies of life.

MUHASABA:
THE EXAMINATION
OF CONSCIENCE
∞

A common practice in Sufism at the outset of a retreat is the examination of conscience, or what is called *Muhasaba*. It is a process of inner scrutiny that requires a high degree of honesty. As difficult as it may be—and one must be very careful, as the mind can be very good at playing games and making up justifications—it is the only way to discover one's real self. Only complete truthfulness leads to clarity of intention. You might begin this process by stepping back from your life and surveying the circumstances you are currently involved in—your relationships, jobs, home, and wider social community. Take time to examine your motives for getting involved in certain activities; explore your expectations of certain people; ask why you initiated certain courses of action.

After scanning your actions and involvements in your personal life, the second step is to examine your overall objective in life. Where does your energy go? What are your ideals? Are you living up to them? These are big questions that you may not immediately know the answers to; indeed, they may arise more naturally during meditations that follow in later chapters. But for now, it is enough just to raise them. What this soul-searching highlights are those things you have given top priority to in your life thus far. Often, for instance, the amount of time allotted to fulfilling your personal survival needs may dramatically outweigh the time devoted to your spiritual needs. This is not uncommon: it takes so much just to survive in our society that there is little time left over to give expression to that which is of most value— creativity, for instance, service to humanity, or spiritual illumination. Yet here it is important to ask yourself how you will feel if you continue living in the same way until the age of ninety or more—for by ignoring the needs of your soul, you run the grave risk of dying in despair.

One way to help initiate a change in direction is to draw up a list of values, then see whether or not you are living up to those values you give top priority to. You might ask yourself, "Am I jeopardizing the higher values for values that are less important? Are those values that I have placed low down on my list—those that don't receive my top priority—still important to me? What really matters?"

You may conclude this initial self-examination by realizing that though you may be deeply entangled in everyday involvements, there is a part of you that, as Christ said, is "in the world but not of the world." In other words, there is a dimension in you that is dedicated to another level of reality than the game of life most people play. It is as if there is a part of you that is a natural hermit, a mystical being who is unwaveringly dedicated to the greatest value in the world: the pursuit of spiritual truth and awakening. It is this part of yourself that you can now open to during the course of your meditation or retreat. Letting go of your personal vantage point—the lens through which you have thus far viewed your life, problems, and values—you step forward into this other world, with the hope that you will return with renewed purpose and insight.

REVERSING DIRECTION

∞

After the examination of conscience, it is time to withdraw your attention from the things of this world, to the world within. Yet often, because your body and psyche may still be set at the rhythm and pace of everyday life, it may be difficult to still your thoughts and focus your attention. Impressions from the outside world may impinge upon your quietude: the television next door, street noise, or disturbing voices. At the same time, random thoughts and feelings may arise from your unconscious, further distracting you. Thus, though you may want to enter into a state of peace and serenity, you may find that you are more agitated than ever. As much as you try to control their effects, you can't. Your will seems useless.

A simple biological principle helps to explain the natural process that is at work. There are two settings of metabolism. One is called the catabolic state, in which the body has been primed since the dawn of time to stay alert and on guard in order to survive. Then there is the anabolic state, where you are in a protected condition and do not need to be on the alert and the rhythm is much slower. When shifting from the catabolic to the anabolic state, there is no better tool than the breath. It is this state of dreamlike reverie, in which the body does not have to respond to external stimuli, that is the optimum condition for meditating. Thus in order to help slow the rhythms of the body and mind, it is best to begin with certain practices that, in effect, place a buffer between the world and yourself in order to allow the unfoldment of your real being. Like a boat trying to cross a choppy sea to reach safe harbor, the purpose of the following practices is to gently guide the practitioner into another dimension of reality that exists just outside of conscious awareness. Rather than will or discipline, music, breath, imagination, and imagery are the means by which we depart the shores of the everyday world, sailing toward distant horizons of unexplored realities.

MUSIC

∞

One method in particular that I find useful in adjusting to a more contemplative mood is listening to a beautiful piece of music. One piece that mirrors the struggle of the psyche to shift rhythms is called "Fratres," on a CD called *Tabula Rasa*. Written by the contemporary composer Arvo Pärt, and played by violin and piano, it begins in a very agitated and energetic rhythm, tries to break the rhythm, and doesn't quite succeed. Then, the music picks up tempo again, this time in a kind of *cri de coeur* that matches the outbreak of deep emotion that can sometimes occur when we meditate. Finally, it slows down, slows down, slows down, easing into a peaceful rhythm, conveying a state of serene beatitude.

THE MIND RIDES THE WIND: ELEMENTAL PURIFICATION BREATHS

∞

When first sitting down to meditate, it is always wise to begin with breathing practices. I suggest that you start by simply being aware of your breath without try-ing to influence it—inhaling, exhaling, inhaling, exhaling. You will find that just being aware of your breath has a calming effect, and slows it down. It's important to know, however, that you are not just drawing in oxygen from the atmosphere and ejecting toxic gases. Rather, the breath is the medium through which you are plugging your own electromagnetic field—the subtle energy body that surrounds and pen-etrates your physical body—into the electromagnetic field of the whole Universe. Thus continue to breathe naturally as you connect to this life energy field. Once you have established a natural rhythm, you can move into the following four breaths, known as the elemen-tal purification breaths that correspond to the four ele-ments: earth, water, fire, and air.

Earth: To attune to the element of earth, first breathe in through the nose and out through the nose. In this stage of the alchemical process of purification, you begin by imagining that, as you exhale, your electro-magnetic force field drains through the bottom of your spine, or the soles of your feet, into Mother Earth. Through this out-breath go all the static gases that have congested your lungs, as well as those heavier ele-ments in your psyche that you would like to be rid of. Just like water down a drain, imagine all your physical and psychological pollution being drawn downward by the powerful gravitational pull of the earth.

Kindly, Mother Earth accepts the dross of your

negative energies through the filter of Her being and recycles it. Thus as you inhale through the nose, imagine that you are drawing in an abundance of fresh energy. Cleared of those things that block you, there is more space within you. A rising buoyancy gives you a sense of being freed of the ballast of those things that have held your spirit down. At the same time, you feel endowed with the positive qualities of the earth: strength, resilience, responsibility, and nurturing. The two names of God to accompany this concentration are *Subhan Allah*, or purity, on the exhalation, and *Muhyi*, or regeneration, on the inhalation.

Water: Next, inhale through the nose and exhale through your mouth. This is the baptism through the element of water. With your lips closed, force the air through your mouth as if you were whistling. This gives you a sense of coolness. As you exhale, it's as if your breath is a shower of water penetrating the very cells of your body. Like an ablution of the Holy Spirit, this descending waterfall of energy washes away all your physical and psychological blocks and impurities. Then, as you inhale, imagine that a fountainhead of pure, artesian springwater is rising up, cleansing and purifiying your being. Because water is malleable and flowing, it endows you with similar qualities of love, compassion, solidarity, and the willingness to cooperate and work with others. Thus the names of God for this breath are *ya Wahabbo*, a stream of flowing water, and *ya Waddud*, love for others.

Fire: In the purification through the element of fire, you breathe in through the mouth, then out through the nose. Rather than identify with your magnetic field, as in the previous concentrations, this practice highlights the bioluminescence of your aura. This is the light that you absorb and transmit back to the environment, so that the body glows like a lamp lit from within. So, as you inhale, imagine that there is a central axis rising like a flame in the spinal cord. You feel that the flame is sucking oxygen out of the environment in order to fuel itself. Through this process, heat is being transformed into light, just as infrared light is transmuted up through the *chakras* in a sequence of colors ranging from red to vermillion, orange, gold, green, blue, violet, ultraviolet, then colorless light.

Then, as you exhale through the nose, feel as if your body has become an incandescent flame and that you are radiating pure light through your heart center. Feel as though you are in a shower of light. Your aura is thoroughly purified of any ambiguity or deviousness by the flame of truth, giving you the courage to stand by what you believe in. The corresponding names of God for the fire breath are *ya Haqq*, or truth, and *ya Nur*, or light.

Air: The last breathing practice is the baptism by air. Here, you breathe in a very refined breath through the mouth, then out through the mouth, and, light as a bird, experience the soaring feeling of unfettered freedom. If you suffer from an addiction of any kind, this is the opportunity to purify your spirit of that gnawing need, releasing it from the prison of desire. Likewise, the air breath emancipates you from those ways of thinking that restrain your soul from exulting in its true nature. As the Sufis say, "Oh, man, if you only knew your freedom; it is your ignorance of your freedom that is your captivity." Liberated from the prison of conditioning, you are free to connect with those ideals you once cherished. Indeed, the idealistic, celestial dimension within you suffers from the limitation of the earthly condition; it needs the nurturing space provided by meditation. Soaring on a cushion of air, you discover modes of thinking that are not based upon ordinary experience, but arise from the ground of Divine intelligence. Eventually, your limited ego is subsumed by the thinking of the Cosmos, restoring it to its relationship to the One and Only Spectator of which it is but an extension. The names of God to repeat here are *ya Wahid*, multiplicity in unity, and *ya Ahid*, oneness.

CULTIVATING DETACHMENT BY TURNING WITHIN

∞

Another method of overcoming distractions while meditating is to repel them through detachment, a practice known as *vairagya* in India. Though detachment is by now a familiar term to many, its deep meaning can be captured through a very powerful image: at the core of our being exists a pure mirror, untarnished and unspoiled by the impressions that fall upon it from the outside world. Like an inborn immunity, this part of us remains consistently whole, innocent, and healthy—even while enduring the numerous involvements and entanglements of this world.

To protect this highly sensitive mirror it is helpful to apply the ancient advice offered by Buddha and imagine that you have placed a sentinel at the doors of perception. Then, imagine that you have surrounded yourself with a wide zone of silence. By this I mean that you must erect a line of defense within the psyche to help you filter the constant intrusions from the outside world: emotions, events in the news, noise from the surrounding environment. Adopting the detached attitude of the ascetic, sort through those thoughts that you feel you can easily "digest," while rejecting those that, for the moment, may be "too big too handle." For example, if an especially troubling issue arises in your mind, just say to yourself, "For the moment, I'm not big enough to handle this. I am only going to allow inside myself those thoughts I am able to easily absorb and attune to." This gives you a feeling of incredible freedom and detachment, not from the world itself, but from your own thoughts and emotions that have kept you tied down.

A further step—the process of transmutation—is helpful in order to deal with intrusive thoughts and emotions. In the same way your digestive system helps you to assimilate certain foods while rejecting others, so, too, does the psyche "digest" impressions. For instance, you peel a vegetable or boil a potato in order to make it more easily digestible. After you eat, your meal becomes part of your system by being broken down and processed by enzymes from the pancreas and the liver. The same is true of psychological impressions from the outer world—they, too, can be broken down, processed, and transmuted inside your psyche. This resembles what psychologists do when helping clients integrate unconscious complexes and emotions.

This practice of detachment can be harmonized with the breath. As you inhale, imagine that all the impressions coming from the outside are being filtered in your psyche. Take, for example, a car accident that, years later, may still preoccupy your mind. At the time it occurred, what stood out may have been facts like the name of the street, the color of the car, or the police report that was filed. Yet over the years those details may have faded, leaving only the quintessence of the situation: the anguish of the person who was hurt, or the guilt of the person responsible for causing the accident. So, as you inhale, you transmute an outer problem by processing it through your filter, then retaining its essential meaning in your psyche. Next, as you hold your breath, center yourself within the core of your being, the untarnished mirror of your soul. As the impressions recorded by this experience or any others glance upon the mirror, imagine that they simply vanish, reabsorbed back into the Universe. Now, there are no more thoughts or emotions, just pure consciousness.

Then, as you exhale, turn toward the outside world once again, only this time it is as if you are approaching it from the inside out, like diving beneath the surface of a lake and glimpsing the network of roots that lie beneath the flowers and plants on its surface. In other words, you are connecting to that level of reality that lies just behind ordinary appearances.

Yoni Mudra: A more advanced breathing practice that further enhances turning one's consciousness within is known as the yogic practice *Yoni Mudra.* Because your awareness is typically oriented outwardly, the idea is to place an obstacle before your consciousness. These blinders cause you to redirect your focus deep inside, so that you may discover a whole world emerging from within. In this concentration, you position your fingers over your lips, nostrils, and eyes as a way to physically block sensations coming from the outside.

To begin, place your index fingers on your eyelids (in such a way that you are not exerting pressure on your eyeballs) and turn your eyeballs upward. Then, place the fourth and fifth fingers on your lips, and the middle fingers on your nostrils. Now, press the middle finger of your left hand and breathe in through the right nostril. Hold your breath, then breathe out through the right nostril. Next, place your thumbs in your ears, and simply do three breaths with your hands in that position. Placing blinders on your eyes shields them from the harsh light of the environment; at the same time, your consciousness turned within discovers an inner light. After these three breaths, take your hands away, maintaining your concentration. Opening your eyes, you may see light emitted by objects around you; closing your eyes, you may feel as if you are seeing light. This is not the radiant light of the sun or stars, but an all-pervading light interspersed like radio waves.

AETHER

Now repeat the same practice, only this time concentrate on inner sound instead of light. As your consciousness turns within, listen closely for the sound of an internal vibration. These vibrations have different frequencies that constitute the language organizing the Universe—what Pythagoras called the symphony of the spheres. This universal sound heard within the peace and silence of your inner chamber is called *Saut-e-Sarmad* by the Sufis. To experience this, you may imagine the sound *hu*—the sound of silence in the pristine stillness of the void from which all creation originally emerged. Then, envision your nervous system as a living musical organ, and imagine your breath blowing this sound through the pipes in your body, filling the whole body with the music of the spheres. To synchronize this concentration on the breath, first inhale, withdrawing from the sounds of the world. Then hold your breath, silently resonating in tune with the all-pervading inner sound. On the exhalation, imagine your breath blowing through the tubes in your body, striking your *chakras* as a hammer strikes a gong, arousing the silent vibrations into audible sound.

PRIMAL

Now, do the practice a third time. This time, as you

hold the breath, concentrate on your solar plexus. Think of it as a gate that opens up into a void where everything is absorbed, then reemerges through the heart in a new way as you exhale. Remember, what you experience when you take your hands away is as important as when your hands are in position. In fact, the whole purpose of *Yoni Mudra* is eventually to be able to do it without physically blocking your senses, in order to redirect your focus inwardly at any time.

DEPTH THINKING

∞

In the previous practices, you have been concentrating on withdrawing from the physical environment. Though sounds, thoughts, and emotions may still arise to distract you, you have learned to displace them to the periphery of your awareness. To avoid being distracted by random thoughts while you remain dimly conscious of this twilight area, your attention is focused like a laser beam on the center of your psyche. Just as in Islam, where the glance is kept straight ahead during the recitation of prayers, you look neither to the left or the right—but inward to the core of your being.

Indeed, as your consciousness descends deeper and deeper, you move from a peripheral mode of thinking toward the creative source of thought itself: *ex nihilo*, out of nothing, come creative thoughts. Here, thought is uninfluenced by language or concepts. Ordinarily when you speak, for instance, you are trying to articulate your thoughts through language. For the most part, the words you use are conventional and reflect the commonplace thinking of your time—this is the case even when you're alone. Hence the reason for maintaining silence on retreat, and not talking while meditating—if you practice remaining speechless for a long enough time, you begin to realize how severely limited your thinking has become through shaping thoughts into the words and concepts of everyday, middle-range consciousness.

In the retreat state, however, you are able to get in touch with a mode of thinking as it emerges from the depths of consciousness. In fact, after a period of time spent meditating, you may find that your way of thinking becomes dramatically different. The physicist David Bohm refers to this as the implicate rather than the explicate state. For instance, thinking in the implicate state would mean intuiting the implications behind thoughts and words, and what we imply behind what we explain outwardly. These thoughts are creative and future-oriented; like portents rising from the depths, they indicate how things could be.

Thus even as distractions arise, the goal is to keep returning to the life source of creative thinking— thoughts that are beyond words and without words. Thus, as you watch thoughts take shape and arise in your mind, begin by observing the assumptions that lie behind them. For instance, when you say "my father," or, when you say that you are suffering, people think they understand what you mean. But your father is a relationship that carries with it a complex web of feelings, and your suffering is a relationship to specific situations, such as the despair that comes from feeling inadequate.

Like an anchor dropped to the ocean floor, what this exercise does is to help shift your concentration from the periphery of consciousness to the depths of your being. This changes how you respond to conditions and disturbances arising in the outside world. Instead of reacting superficially, or cutting it out altogether, you respond from a very deep place inside yourself. One of the best illustrations I have for explaining this dynamic is found in Beethoven's Fourth Piano Concerto. With this piece, Beethoven portrays the world's cry of agony through an orchestral movement. This is followed by one of the most beautiful piano melodies Beethoven ever composed. To me, this was a musical expression of his deep response—rather than an automatic, reflexive reaction—to the world's endless pain and suffering. His piano melody was a wordless response to the cries of agony from the depth of his being, rather than a mere reaction from the periphery of his consciousness.

THROUGH THE DOORWAY OF THE IMAGINATION

Like a doorway opening to that which transpires behind that which appears, an image can also help lead the psyche into the landscape of the soul. For instance, after soothing your emotions through listening to a beautiful piece of music, slowing the rhythm of the body through various breathing practices, then shifting your focus from the periphery to the inner depths of consciousness, you may wish to enter a more deeply meditative state where visual images may serve as a bridge between two worlds.

Imagine, for instance, that you have stumbled upon what looks like a high wall guarding an ancient temple. Unlatching an old, ornately decorated gate set in a stone wall, you find yourself entering an enchanted emerald garden. Though this secret haven seems absolutely impenetrable, it is shielded entirely by a zone of silence that protects against invasion. Once inside, you stroll among the flowers and trees in a very tranquil state; here, you are free to enter into a communion with nature. Everything appears absolutely transfigured, effulgent with the presence of the Divine. Guarded against the intrusion of disturbing thoughts, you settle down to contemplate, securely ensconced within your peaceful inner garden.

There is another visualization that helps to shift consciousness: lying in bed, perhaps in the early morning hours of dawn, hover in the liminal state between waking and dreaming. In this reverie, a succession of mythic images may flash across the screen of your mind. At the same time, remain conscious of the furniture in your room and the sensations of your body. If you were to control these images as they arise, you would immediately be thrown back into ordinary consciousness; likewise, if you were to plunge more deeply into them, you would fall asleep. The trick is to allow yourself to hover in that threshold state in which the collective unconscious erupts in the form of pictures and images. Dreamlike reverie is very important in setting the stage for meditation, as it helps to cultivate a receptive condition to altered states of consciousness.

A further visualization is to imagine that you're walking along the shores of a lake in the moonlight. Somehow, you've managed to leave your life behind; few thoughts trouble your mind. Barely a breeze stirs the surface of the water; it's as still as glass. A misty haze hangs over the evening landscape, and a diaphanous light is reflected upon the lake's placid stillness. As you continue walking around the lake, you feel soothed by an abiding sense of calm. Something within you seems to share the same nature as this enchanted scene. Indeed, your heavy, physical body now feels spun of a more subtle, gossamerlike fabric. You feel as though you are floating on a cushion of air above the ground, walking very lightly in a state of beautiful equanimity.

Finally, you may want to try a visualization that begins with the question "Who am I—really?" It's as if there is a layer of memory hidden in your psyche that calls out to be excavated. You can remember, for instance, what it felt like to be a child, or even an infant. Perhaps you may even be able to summon up the memory of being in your mother's womb, or, reaching further back, the "perinatal" states of consciousness prior to conception described by the transpersonal psychiatrist Dr. Stanislav Grof. However, if you can't excavate those layers of the unconscious, then I find that it helps to imagine yourself as a visitor from outer space who has landed on planet earth.

In this meditation, you feel as if you are a visitor to earth. It isn't your real place of origin, just a temporary home away from home. Because you have taken up residence here, the planet has provided you with a physical vehicle, the body, woven of the fabric of your parents and ancestors. Over the course of your lifetime here, however, the memory of your other home has slowly faded away. Looking back, you see how you became more and more entangled in situations and relationships, and how your identity became narrowed down by the outer environment. You see how you have become shaped by the challenges you have been forced to deal with: the joy, pain, and suffering of existence. Now, however, in this meditation, you want to reverse the direction you have been moving in since birth. You want to recover the memory of your true identity. You want to remember your real place of origin.

To begin this recovery process, you begin to sense that you have imprinted the hallmark of your eternal being beyond time, space, and form upon the fabric of your body, which is a necessary underpinning in order to survive as part of human civilization. Though you can't entirely separate yourself from it, you know that it is less essentially who you are than the supercelestial being you really are. Just realizing that you have some-how forgotten this part of yourself suffices to awaken a dim memory of other spheres of consciousness. For when I say that you are not from planet earth, what I really mean is that you are descended from levels of reality other than the one you normally take for granted.

As this realization dawns, you feel the environment slowly begin to recede from view. Your sense of bodi-ness lightens; even the contours of your face convey something of your true nature transpiring through them. Likewise, you see, how your personality is a hoax—a mask covering your real self. In fact, what you think you were, you now see, is merely something that accrued during the course of your incarnation, like the husks of a kernel of wheat stripped during harvest. Now that you have downplayed these perishable and transient aspects of your being—your body, your thoughts, and your personality—there is no limit to the potentialities and possibilities lying in wait. Free, you soar toward your Divine homeland. There, you feel the ecstasy of reuniting with your original being— which you forgot you really were and which you repre-sent as your Divine Mother and Divine Father.

Indeed, whether you know it or not, in everyday life you are, for the most part, playing a role and wearing a mask. The mistake you make is that you identify with the mask you see when looking in the mirror—a sec-ondary aspect of yourself that reflects but a fraction of the richness of your essential being. As you begin to experience freedom from attachments during the course of a retreat, however, the real being behind the role you've been playing all along begins to dawn in your consciousness. You realize, "Yes, I'm a housewife, or a doctor, or a typist, but that's not all of who I am— that's my outer condition." The real breakthrough comes when you discover the celestial countenance lying just behind your physical face. That is your real face, your cosmic face, and it's incredibly beautiful—it could perhaps be the face of a young person with no wrinkles, or the face of a very mature being in a young body. But whatever its configuration, it isn't difficult to recognize: when you come across it, something clicks and you know with instant certainty, "This is me." Gradually, the difference between the mask you have worn every day and your true being begins to fade, and the beauty of your soul begins to transpire through your whole being.

At this stage, it is important to remind meditators that these practices and those that follow are not just intended to help us rediscover our true, essential nature—but also the entirely new being we are becoming through our evolutionary journey on earth. This is where Sufism, particularly the teachings of Hazrat Inayat Khan, has something different to contribute to the spirituality of our time. In Sufism, there is a strong sense of the uniqueness of each person. The body and the personality are important inasmuch as they are able to accurately reflect this being-in-the-process-of-becoming. Thus rather than trying to escape life because you are nothing more than the victim of circumstances, through your meditations you begin to discover instead that you are indeed a significant part of the overall plan—with an important mission and purpose to carry out.

THREE

ATTUNING TO THE MASTERS, SAINTS, AND PROPHETS

"Spiritual attainment is attuning oneself to a higher pitch."

— HAZRAT INAYAT KHAN

◆

As a young man during the decades following World War II, I became passionately engaged in a search for living exemplars of spiritual realization. Venturing far and wide, I sought out, in addition to the dervishes, Hindu yogis and *rishis*, as well as Buddhist and Christian monks. Of the many ascetics I encountered on this quest, most, in my estimation, ultimately failed to pass the test of authenticity. Some, it seemed, derived satisfaction from exercising power over seekers; others were very skilled in the art of sophisticated

67

trickery—and little else—while still others became renowned simply because they attracted increasingly larger audiences. Yet the absence of true mystical depth on the part of so many only served to make my encounters with the rare beings of true enlightenment that much more powerful. In their presence I felt uplifted, as if I were "walking on air." The effects of their realization upon others was palpable; their inner sovereignty was so great that they were able to help people gain their self-confidence.

Indeed, it is true that the attunement of another person can help shift consciousness in a way that a person cannot do on his or her own. For while we may say that ultimately God is our only guru, or the Universe our guide, there are times when the circumstances of life can be so overwhelming that we may need the assistance of another. Especially in the beginning of the spiritual journey, learning to shift from the earthly perspective to the Divine perspective is not something that happens immediately. The skill of integrating one's individual identity and personal vantage point with that of the Divine is the culmination of a contemplative process that unfolds slowly over time, and only after much practice and discipline. That is why, down through the ages, the support and guidance of a teacher has proved invaluable, providing she or he is authentic.

Especially today, however, it is often the case that trustworthy and experienced spiritual guides are difficult to find. Yet the Sufis have a longstanding practice that provides an antidote to this modern dilemma: turning to humankind's great masters, saints, or prophets such as Moses, Krishna, Jesus, Kuan Yin, Zoroaster, Melchizedek, Muhammad, and others. They form a hierarchy of mystical transmission reaching into the very highest levels of realization announcing the spiritual dimension of our day and age and indeed future spirituality. Hazrat Inayat Khan invites us to concentrate on all the masters, saints, and prophets of the past; in this way, we are building a bridge of our thoughts and attunements to these beings that enables them to support and guide us.

The spiritual practice of getting into the consciousness of an illuminated being—one of the archangels, masters, saints, sages, prophets, or dervishes who since the beginning of time has embodied the universal spirit of Divine guidance—is called *tawajjuh* by the Sufis, which is attunement instead of imaging. One cannot transform oneself through willpower. Rather, just as a violinist, cellist, or harpsichordist will tune to a certain pitch before playing, meditation is a matter of calibrating one's emotional and mental vibrations. Just like tuning the strings of a violin to a note struck on the piano, concentrating on an "ideal being" has the effect of harmonizing that within us which has fallen out of tune with the Divine perspective. While our own spiritual dimension may be latent within us, that of certain great souls is vibrantly awakened.

Getting in the consciousness of highly attuned beings will trigger off a kind of resonance in us—just as two harps tuned to the same pitch will strike the same chord.

In addition, entering into the consciousness of one of the world's great masters allows us to see the circumstances of our own life from their expanded and enhanced point of view, enabling us to view certain difficult situations in a way we wouldn't have seen otherwise. Turning the prism of consciousness, we can also see how that being sees those Divine Qualities within us that we may have lost sight of in the fog of everyday life and allow us to reconfigure ourselves according to that upgraded perception.

∞

There are three steps that form the basis of this practice. The first is representing to ourselves an image of a prophet, master, or saint as he or she has come down to us through history. The message of Sufism today points to the importance of the spirituality of the future calling upon understanding and integrating into a meaningful pattern the essential contributions of the world religions. I therefore recommend choosing three teachers from different traditions. Concentrations can be done on each one successively, while observing closely exactly how the thought of a particular master or prophet influences one's attunement. Initially, we may think of a particular teacher in the context of the time period during which he or she lived—the civilization in which Buddha lived, for instance, was very different from that of Abraham. Gradually, however, the intention is to deepen our connection to a particular prophet in a way that goes far beyond the ordinary time they lived in—even imagining how they might be today. Shiva, for example, might be teaching people how to overcome illness through mastery, while Buddha might be the most eminent psychotherapist of our time. Abraham and Muhammad would form a coalition to show the underlying unity of all religions—perhaps fulfilling the role of High Commissioners of the Congress of Religions. Christ would probably be in a prison camp in compassionate solidarity with the victims of political abuse and oppression.

Freeing particular saints or prophets from the constraints of the cultures in which they were born leads us to the second stage of this practice—grasping the inner meaning and essence of the illuminated beings who have appeared through the ages. Instead of attuning to the historical Jesus, we think instead of the Cosmic Christ, or Buddha *Tathagata* instead of Siddhartha Gautama. As has been stressed by virtually all of the major religions, whether Hinduism, Buddhism, Judaism, or Islam, the image of a prophet or saint can only be a stepping-stone toward a direct relationship with the Divine. Islam warns against the danger of idolatry, teaching instead that there are three stages of concentration. In a first stage, one loses oneself in the thought of a master; this is called *fana-*

fi-sheikh. In a second step, one loses oneself in the contemplation of a prophet, such as Muhammad, or *fana-
fi-rasoul*. This leads to a third stage in which one loses
oneself in the Divine Consciousness, or *fana-fi-Allah*.

Thus the Sufis teach concentrating on an illuminated being by entering into their consciousness as
deeply as possible—to the point that we imagine what
it is like to be that particular sage or mystic, as well as
to imagine the particular Divine Quality each one
embodies. Shiva, for instance, represents the overcoming of the frailties of the human condition. Muhammad
represents the Divine Power; Abraham represents the
Divine Sovereignty. The essence of the Virgin Mary is
our soul in its utmost purity—the immaculate state
that reflects back to us our own celestial counterpart,
or our higher selves.

In fact, when we contemplate the wealth of Divine
Qualities as they manifest through these timeless
teachers, a kind of mirroring effect takes place in which
we are able to discover the very same potentialities
latent in our being that are displayed in the prophet,
master, or saint we are meditating upon. Like the sun
breaking through clouds, the splendor of Buddha's
enlightenment liberates us from the prison of illusion,
freeing our souls. Christ's compassion melts away the
hatred and resentment that freezes the heart, allowing
our own compassion to bubble forth once again. And
Muhammad gives us self-confidence in the Divine
Power that erupts within us when we glorify God in
His majesty.

The following meditations on some of humankind's most magnificent teachers are culled from my own inner experiences of these rare beings, and are intended as a guide to individuals' own meditative encounters with God's great emissaries.

SHIVA

∞

In traditional Hindu mythology, Shiva is pictured sitting on Mount Kalais—a high peak in the vastness of a mountain landscape. Seated on a tiger skin in meditative repose, he has a cobra wrapped around his neck and a trident in his hands. This pose symbolizes Shiva's ability to develop mastery over outer conditions, and his capacity to discipline the furtive mind and emotions such as pain, horror, dismay, or joy that may stand in the way of mastery. The *rishis*, those who continue Shiva's tradition, harden their bodies by means of the most stressful conditions imaginable: burning heat, cold, hunger, fasting, exhaustion, and staying awake through the night. Ironically, practicing this extreme physical discipline produces an exalted sense of euphoria—just as when we discipline ourselves by giving up something we want for the sake of our ideal a kind of exaltation overtakes us, and raises consciousness—unlike the results of permissiveness or laziness.

The name of God for attuning to Shiva is *ya Wali*, to which can be added *ya Qadr*. *Wali* means mastery, and *Qadr* means the release of Divine power. These names of God do not serve to inflate one's ego by strengthening one's personal control or will, but instead evoke a dimension of our being that is archetypal and superpersonal in nature. It would be like attuning to the majesty of a thunderstorm as it passes over a range of mountain peaks, or the strength of an ancient, gigantic redwood. Furthermore, it is important to point out that every Divine Quality has its shadow side, and that it is precisely because of our fear of falling into the shadow that we have difficulty developing a particular quality. The shadow side of mastery, for instance, would be ruthlessness or selfish manipulation. By continually remembering the connection between one's individual will and the Divine source of power, however, one is able to prevent falling into the flow of despotism, or autocratically wielding one's personal will over others.

Having represented to our imagination the traditional image of Shiva, let us let go of that form, delving even deeper into his consciousness. Can you put yourself in a frame of mind, for instance, in which you have completely conquered your addictions or shortcomings through mastering the most incredible physical discomfort, nervous stress, and emotional loneliness? Can you imagine what it would be like to be completely segregated from the world, living entirely alone in a cave for ten or twelve years? Gradually, this would give us a glimpse of what it feels like to have totally overcome the limitations of life. The combination of this winged detachment and powerful self-discipline awakens within us the qualities of mastery and power: the twin pillars necessary to fulfill the Divine Purpose for which each of us was born.

BUDDHA

∞

The image of the Buddha is so embedded in the collective unconscious that pictures of this teacher of serenity arise easily: sitting cross-legged in peaceful stillness beneath a tree, or walking among his fellow monks radiating luminosity, peace, and deep concern for the suffering of humanity. Discarding the wealth and royal position into which he was born, he realized that the only thing that was meaningful to him was the attainment of a state of freedom from conditioning leading to awakening. He showed contempt for those things of the world. Breaking radically from the commonplace life of earning a living or raising a family, Buddha practiced absolute one-pointedness, going through the most painful asceticism—even to the extent of having to crawl on all fours in order to get to water, covered with vermin and weakened to the point that he was as thin as a skeleton. He took long retreats in a cave; later he sat beneath the Bodhi tree for a period of forty days without eating or sleeping—and in those days, the place was surrounded by wild animals, insects, and venomous snakes. Yet he kept to his vow, undeterred, until he discovered the steps that led to the attainment of illumination and enlightenment.

Despite his nearly superhuman efforts to rise above the demands of ordinary life, Buddha ultimately discovered that those kinds of hardships did not in themselves catalyze spiritual awakening. Yet there is a symbolic wisdom to be found in the pattern of his life story: when consciousness is lifted beyond the vantage point of the individual ego, it becomes cosmic.

Thus when we remove the historical layer surrounding Buddha, and attempt to enter into the consciousness of this great being, we begin by attuning to a mood of detachment. Can you imagine, for instance, as I have done, meditating under the Bodhi tree in India all night long? Almost immediately one is swept by the sensation of a tremendous expanse of space that continues to move outward in an ever-widening immensity. Surrounded by this zone of silence, one is protected from the distractions of the immediate environment. There is a feeling of sitting quietly in a temple. The temple in which one is sitting is without walls, encircled by an invisible boundary that divides the sacred from the profane. This boundary is created by the Buddha's innate sense of detachment: like a peaceful moat dividing the castle from the outside world, the result of this detachment is an abiding sense of serenity and peace undisturbed by the incessant demands of the world. From this emotionally detached perspective of Buddha's consciousness, we feel raised beyond existence itself, and are granted a marvelous overview of life on earth. Like a mythic bird, we can fly far beyond the planet, the solar system, the galaxy, and even beyond into the farthest reaches of the Universe. This symbolic flight of the soul, however, has nothing to do with actual space, but represents further dimensions of reality—a pitch of consciousness that continually ascends to ever higher and higher notes of awareness. Indeed, when the mind is liberated from illusory desires and transient concerns, consciousness is set free. This is what Buddha meant when he illustrated consciousness with a flame—if there is no log to burn, the flames eventually die down. In the same way, our ego-consciousness depends upon an object to sustain its attachments. Deprived of an object, it is released from the limitations of earthly existence into boundaryless, transcendent intelligence, or what the Buddha called "beyond consciousness, beyond existence and non-existence."

These clues to the consciousness of the Buddha awaken in one an awareness of freedom, and the discovery of another dimension of existence that is unbound, unfettered, and freed from the narrow conditioning of our personal identity. This is what is behind the words of Buddha at the end of his retreat at the Bodhi tree when he said, "I have overcome conditioning," or, as he calls it, "the freedom from deter-

minism." Thus if we have a sense of Buddha's attunement, it will awaken within us the need for the freedom that is so often constricted by everyday
responsibilities. In this way, the example of Buddha
shows the steps to attaining enlightenment and, ultimately, liberation from suffering.

ZOROASTER

Shrouded in the mists of history is Zoroastrianism, the
Mazdaic tradition, an ancient path where illumination
is attained through being inspired by the light that can
be found in nature, such as the light of the stars. The
transmission through the ages from prophet to prophet
describes Zoroaster, the founder of this tradition of
light, as a Magus: a kingly, luminous being. His mission is to dissolve the veil between the earthly plane and
the celestial planes of variously unfolding levels of
light. As in Dante's vision of the heavenly spheres,
these dimensions of light are formed of infinite hierarchies of angels and archangels, singing and radiating
their praise of the Divine. The accompanying names of
God we use for this attunement are *ya Nur*, light, and
ya Quddus, holiness.

According to the teachings of Zoroaster, it is light
that overcomes deceit, lying, ambiguity, and manipulation—all those things that lurk in the darkness.
Much of this darkness exists because, like creatures

blind to the splendor that surrounds us, we live in a flattened universe devoid of all its bounty. We do not see, as Zoroaster taught, that there is "beingness" in matter. Water, for instance, is not just H_2O that pours out of the faucet—it is the body of a spiritual being, the archangel Ardvisura Anahita. Asking permission of Ardvisura to partake of her gifts when we swim or bathe opens up an entirely different perspective on the world of nature. It is a perspective that encourages respect for the purity of water, rather than following our greed in polluting the planet's rivers, streams, and oceans.

Likewise the earth itself, according to the tradition of Zoroaster, is the body, or the crystallization, of the archangel Zamiat. Thus we extend the praise and respect we feel for Zamiat to the sanctity of animals, as well as the spiritual status of all living creatures. Through this attunement to the prophet Zoroaster, we enter into a resonance with the one true being who is concealed behind the appearance of all the wondrous, myriad forms of material reality.

ABRAHAM
AND MELCHIZEDEK

The Old Testament prophet Abraham is a being who plays a very important part in the religious thinking of the West. According to the descriptions that have come down to us through history, we imagine him to be a patriarch, a giant of a man, a grandfatherly figure with a towering personality. If we get into his consciousness, an imperative wells up to more keenly attune to Abraham's greater authority in the midst of our day-to-day lives.

To begin our meditation on the being of the patriarch Abraham, we might try to think what it was like to live as he did 3,700 years ago, wandering in the desert. The silence and loneliness would be deafening; from one moment to the next, a fluttering breeze could turn into a violently howling tempest. This primitive desert solitariness enhanced the presence of an invisible reality that Abraham attuned to, making him open to receive messages to give guidance to his people. This message was not for himself alone, but for his entire community, indeed, for the whole of humanity.

Abraham's prophetic attunement as an ambassador of the one and only Being contrasts with the state of *samadhi* that is detached from the human condition, as embodied by Shiva. It stems instead from a great sense of responsibility for one's fellow human beings—not a contempt for the world that breeds seclusion and asceticism.

The sovereignty of Abraham, however, is secular in comparison to the authority of Melchizedek—the high priest who crowned Abraham as king. Melchizedek is recognized by Judaism, Christianity, and Islam, and thus represents a religious authority whom they each have in common. No doubt he sacrificed at the altar in Jerusalem, which is probably the stone now housed in the Dome of the Rock. I believe he must have lived in the cave that is at the top of the Mount of Olives—a place where I once took a retreat—whereas most of his people at the time were living in tents. When I imagine the being of Melchizedek, I think of him as very, very holy, with a personality that is totally dedicated to attuning to the sacred. Thus his authority is quite different from that of Abraham's. Can you, for instance, put yourself back in time to that moment when Melchizedek, during a ceremony in which bread and wine were offered as a sacrament, anointed Abraham as king? It is a moment of Divine transmission, in which Melchizedek conferred upon Abraham God's blessings as His ambassador on earth.

What do we find when we enter deeply into the consciousness of both Abraham and Melchizedek? In the contours of their historical story, we discover the essence of the interrelationship that exists between the sacred and the secular forms of authority. In the very highest sense, these two powers should always be interdependent. You could say, for instance, that Abraham represents a prototype of what government should be. He had to lay down the law and give prescriptions to people that were relevant to the needs of his time. Indeed, people in all times need guidance through the tribulations of life—preferably from someone with a genuine sense of Divine authority rather than personal ego power. But on an even deeper level, Abraham signifies the quality of inner authority. It is conveyed in the name of God *ya Qahr*, or Divine sovereignty. Thus in attuning to the being of Abraham, or in the repetition of the name of God *ya Qahr*, we discover within ourselves the propensity for authority linked with discipline.

But for this authority to be complete, it must be imbued with a sense of the sacred, symbolized here by Abraham's relationship to the High Priest Melchizedek. Abraham's assumption of the awesome responsibility of steering human destiny could only remain on course when it was connected up to its source in the Holiest of Holies—the role that Melchizedek symbolized. In fact, this authority is inextricably derived from sacredness. Though subtle, the quality of sacredness is something we feel, for instance, when we enter the precincts of a church, mosque, temple, or synagogue. Within the boundaries of such a sanctuary, we feel protection from the sacrilege of profanity—from all the harshness, defilement of the spirit, lack of respect, and covetousness that riddles everyday life. The name of God that most closely conveys a sense of the sacred is *ya Quddus*. It is an attunement to that which is undefiled within our souls; in order to honor that attunement to the sacred, we need to express it in the form of orderliness, discipline, authority, and patronage. Thus when the two powers, authority and sacredness, or *ya Qahr/ya Quddus* are yoked together in an authentic way, then individual authority is protected from deteriorating into willful selfishness. In turn, the strength of our inner authority protects the sacred element at the core of our being.

CHRIST

∞

In our time we are beginning to have access to two dimensions of Jesus Christ: the historic Jesus and the Cosmic Christ. While the Cosmic Christ is beyond time and space and becoming, the human, historic Jesus represents a certain development within the Jewish tradition. While we all know the familiar parables of the three wise men, the shepherds, and the star, the central fact that is important to remember is that Jesus was a rebel and a pioneer in his time. Another important factor to remember about Jesus is that he had his novitiate in the Essene Order.

The Essene Order was an esoteric organization structured along initiatic grades, or the degree of spiritual realization to which an individual had attained. It was part of a lineage of authentic mystical traditions originating among the Zoroastrians in Iran. At a certain time there must have been a revolution within the Essene Order, because St. John the Baptist, also a member, recognized Jesus as the Master of righteousness they were awaiting. He opened the door from that hier-

archical, initiatic order to a world religion by declar-
ing, "But many that are first shall be last and the last
shall be first." But had he stayed and become the head
of that order, his world mission would never have been
fulfilled.

Both St. John the Baptist and Jesus became out-
casts. In those days it was very difficult to survive
because there was no asylum in any home for those out-
casts from the Essenes. In the alienation and loneliness
of the desert, however, John developed great inner
magnetism that drew many people to his being, and
through him, to Christ. He baptized in water those
who flocked to him: an initiation that marked a commitment to following the spiritual ideal.

Even in these sparsely known details of the life of
Jesus, we can see the origins of the unique hallmark of
his teachings—teachings that ultimately were to prove
totally revolutionary and unconventional, even demo-
cratic. Instead of overcoming the body and mind
through mastery, for instance, Jesus washes the feet of
his disciples and sits in the tavern with drunkards. He
honors and protects an adulteress, saying, "Let he who
is without sin cast the first stone." Some of his pro-
nouncements are very challenging and provocative. For
example, he went so far as to say, "I could destroy the
Temple and build it again."

Perhaps he spoke words that didn't appear to make
sense because people were suffering from living under
the iron rule of the Romans, like France under the

Nazis. When confronted by people about how they should respond to the rules and stiff taxes imposed by the Romans, he responded, "Give to Caesar what belongs to Caesar and to God what belongs to God." Thus instead of introducing another kingdom, which would have been challenging to the secular kingdom of the Jews and the Roman Empire, Jesus was promising the Kingdom of Heaven. Furthermore, instead of saying "leave the world," as did the ascetics, he said to be "in the world but not of the world." That was something very new, a real departure from mystical tradition. The prophetic mission of Israel was to bring the law to the people. Jesus preached the way of love and forgiveness (*tiphereth*, in the Kabbalah).

How do we enter into the consciousness of the being of the Cosmic Christ? We can begin by focusing our consciousness on the image of Christ as portrayed on the Shroud of Turin. While a lot of controversy surrounds the authenticity of the shroud, still, I am convinced that this is the real Christ. Rather than the blond, blue-eyed man romanticized in certain images of Jesus, the Shroud of Turin portrays a strong "superbeing." Indeed, if we look very deeply into this image, it leads us into a gigantic status of the human dimension that reaches beyond the limits of ordinary humanness. From this place, we might, perhaps, begin to attune to the suffering of Jesus when he was enduring his hour of darkness at the Garden of Gethsemane, when, foreseeing what the next day would bring, he tried to arouse his disciples to be with him. But they were all sleeping. It is still like that. Christ is still calling, inviting us into his consciousness, and others like him, who might be enduring moments of utter abandonment and despair.

Understanding the depths of Jesus' own suffering in that historic moment allows us to grasp the essence of what to me was his ultimate message: "Blessed are the poor in spirit." A more recent translation of this Beatitude is "Be of good cheer, those of you who are forlorn in life." Thus the message of Jesus Christ was aimed directly at those who are floundering in life, or who are poor, sick, or dejected. That includes the wound within us of the lack of self-worth and rejected vulnerability. The very last scene of Jesus' life on earth—the Crucifixion—was seemingly a terrible fiasco. His disciples didn't have the courage to admit that they were his disciples. They were frightened of the violence of the Romans—and many of them were the same people who had cheered him on the Mount of Olives. So superficial was people's loyalty that when they saw him on the cross they taunted him, saying, "Ha!—he said he could give us life eternal. . . . He can't even save himself." The fact that he couldn't save himself, in their limited vision, made all that had gone before a hoax.

Yet that fiasco turned out to be one of the greatest victories the world has ever known. What seemed to be only a crucifixion turned out to be a coronation—but one would have had to see through the eyes of God in order to witness it. Look at it from yet another angle. Instead of Christ saying, "Why have you abandoned me?" how would it be if he was speaking with the voice of God, saying to the people, "Why have you abandoned me?" Here we have the whole human drama encapsulated in one dramatic vignette: the desperate soul-searchings, sufferings, and tribulations intrinsic to the human condition. That is exactly why the crucifixion of Christ became seared into the collective imagination—the way the image of the resurrected Christ burned itself into the Shroud of Turin—impressing itself into the souls of millions of human beings since that time. And it is why the message of Jesus Christ became cosmic, embodying the mystical truth that the suffering of each individual is not only personal, but cosmic in dimension.

Indeed, as we go even more deeply into Christ Consciousness, we can find within ourselves that place of crucifixion or failure, something which resonates with Christ's struggle. Perhaps our own self-esteem has been quashed and usurped in some way by the powers that be—those self-appointed judges of conscience who are members of institutionalized religion. Like Christ, the authenticity of our being suffocates under the constraint of any effort to institutionalize one's real spiritual experience and attunement. Just imagine, for example, what happened centuries later to Joan of Arc within the very tradition of Christianity itself. She was

a young peasant girl; her accusers were learned digni-
taries. Faced with what appeared to be their overwhelming authority compared to her own ignorance, at
one point the darkness of doubt beclouded her conviction and she recanted. Ultimately, however, she clung
to her faith and the authenticity of those visions. At this
point she was burned at the stake.

This story of suffering and crucifixion is an all-too-
frequent narrative that occurs again and again throughout the course of history. Such was the case during
World War II with the Nazis and the Jews; even today
in countries around the world, people at this very
moment are being tortured or killed for their beliefs.
This was the tragic fate of my own sister, Noor, who
was tortured to death in a German concentration camp
as a result of her work for the French underground.
It is in the very depths of the despair of such beings
that we find the living Christ, standing in compassionate solidarity with the downtrodden and the
oppressed. His message speaks to each person who
strives to uphold the voice of conscience in the face of
those who attempt to impose their will upon
us. Indeed, the quest for freedom in our time is leading
to the realization that nobody can make us what we
are not, or take away who we are, in the essence of
our being.

MUHAMMAD

∞

The Prophet Muhammad laid no claim to be of Divine origin. He was born to parents who were merchant-class Meccans. Muhammad's father died before he was born, while his mother died when he was six—leaving him orphaned at a very young age. Despite these difficult beginnings, Muhammad grew up to become a mighty, kingly figure, a great political reformer, a lawgiver, and a prophet. Indeed, his most significant contribution to humanity was the Holy Qur'an: a Divine revelation he began to receive while on retreat in a cave on the mountain of Hira. This revelation was received by Muhammad in a series of messages he identified as the voice of the Archangel Gabriel. Even despite this miraculous event, Muhammad did not wish to be deified—as Krishna, for example, had been deified by the Hindus as an *avatar*—but said simply that he had been delegated as a messenger of God.

Although Muhammad performed no physical miracles—such as curing illnesses or making food appear—he performed the incredible feat of uniting the warring tribes of the Hijaz in the seventh century. Overcoming the legacy of bitter vendetta, vandalism, blood orgies, and the worship of pagan gods that characterized these fractious tribes, Muhammad helped to create one of the greatest civilizations in history. Indeed, over time, Islamic scholars became renowned for their contributions to the fields of art, mathemat-

ics, astronomy, and philosophy. In addition, Muhammad's sense of mission to restore and protect the
religion of Abraham led him to safeguard several sacred places of pilgrimage from profiteering and
idolatry: the Ka'bah, a cubical shrine inset in its eastern corner with the Black Stone (probably a meteorite);
the Maqam Abraham, the place from which the
Prophet Abraham was believed to have prayed toward
the Ka'bah; and the Zamzam well, where pilgrims
come to drink water that is said to have sacred proper-
ties. As Hazrat Inayat Khan said of Muhammad,
"When asked, 'Where is He? Is He in our temples? Is
He in the Ka'bah?' he said, 'No, His temple is in man's
heart.' "

Muhammad was among the earliest pioneers of the
era of religious democracy. He eschewed any interces-
sion between man and God, advocating no priesthood
and affirming the possibility of direct dialogue
between man and God in prayer.

Speaking of the different prophets and masters of
the past, Hazrat Inayat Khan had this to say with
regard to the Prophet Muhammad: "This work was
thus continued by all the prophets until Muhammad,
the Khatim al Mursalin, the last messenger of Divine
wisdom and the seal of the prophets, came on his mission, and in his turn gave the final statement of Divine
wisdom: 'None exists but Allah.' This message fulfilled
the aim of his prophetic mission. The prophecy of
Muhammad was: 'Now that all the world has received
the message through a man who is subject to all limi-

tations and conditions of human life, the message will in the future be given without claim.' "

Those who would like to use one of the names of God to attune to the Prophet Muhammad can recite the phrase *Dhul Jelal wal Ikram*, the Lord of Splendor and Sovereignty.

FOUR

BECOMING
A BEING OF LIGHT

"I emanated upon thee a force of love so that
thou mayest be fashioned according to My
glance."

— Qur'an

"I saw myself through the light that things
carry in their essence—not through any extra-
neous light."

— IBN 'ARABI

"As the eyes cannot see themselves, so it is
with the soul—it is sight itself. The moment
it closes its eyes, its own light manifests to its
view."

— HAZRAT INAYAT KHAN

*"The soul in its manifestation on the earth is
not at all disconnected to the higher spheres. It
lives in all the spheres, although it generally
is only conscious of one level. Only a veil sepa-
rates us. The seer's own soul becomes a torch in
his hand. It is his own light that illuminates
his path. It is just like directing a searchlight
into dark corners which one could not see
before."*

— HAZRAT   INAYAT   KHAN

❖

When I was living in the caves in the Himalayas, I
would arise in the early hours before dawn and meditate on the otherworldly light that illuminates the
horizon just before the sun rises. Then, during the
daytime, I would spend hours looking into the sun. As
the Greek philosopher Plotinus said, "To look into the
sun, I have to have eyes like the sun." And last, at
night, I would meditate on the stars. Closing my eyes,
I would reach right out into the lacy-bright nebulae,
seeing my body as a fragment within the vastness of
infinitely revolving worlds of light.

Light is a particularly important factor in spiritual
unfolding because it acts as a bridge between matter
and the ineffable dimensions that lie just beyond our
immediate perception. Indeed, the scientific phenomenon of light gives us a clue into the age-old enigma
that the nature of reality cannot be entirely explained
by what we see with our eyes alone. For example, most

people consider their consciousness as a focal point located in time and space. Similarly, physical light seems to radiate from specific locations in space—the sun, the stars, a candle, or an electric lightbulb. Yet when meditators turn within, they often experience a more diffuse consciousness. Hazrat Inayat Khan calls this the "all-pervading light." Ibn 'Arabi, as well, says, "Light is of two kinds: a light having no rays and radiant light."

Like mystics, physicists never cease to be amazed by the paradoxical nature of light. When they try to measure it in laboratory experiments, they can only ascertain what happens at the instant it interacts with their instruments—for light resists giving any clues to its behavior before, after, or between measurements. As this example illustrates, light can hardly be classified as matter: for even though it is an electromagnetic phenomenon, unlike any other form of matter it does not have mass. Thus the remarkable thing is that light itself provides us with a useful model exemplifying the interconnection between energy and matter—or, the uncreated Universe and the created Cosmos. Just like light, for example, reality escapes any efforts on our part to track it down beyond the existential world we commonly know. From this vantage point, what we call reality begins to look more like the cross-section of a multiple, multi-dimensional, and many-tiered Universe. And the further we go in attempting to define it, the more reality appears as a virtuality that becomes an actuality in the existential condition.

FASHIONING
A BODY OF LIGHT
∞

Concentrating on the physical light in the surrounding environment is a wonderful introduction to light practices. I recommend beginning with a walk in nature, while being conscious of the fluorescing light reflecting off the trees, flowers, and even the tiniest blade of grass. When touching the leaf of a tree or flower, you can envision the subtle sensation of light that is emitted from your hands as it commingles with the plants' auras. Indeed, the purpose of these practices with visible manifestations of light in the surrounding environment is to discover the light suffusing the physical body. Our physical bodies, along with every other piece of matter in the Cosmos, originated in the Big Bang— that incredible, primordial explosion of radiant light that eventually crystallized into matter. You could imagine, for instance, that your body is like light that has jelled into liquid crystal. Or, you could think of yourself as a biological crystal that has the extraordinary faculty of absorbing light from the environment and being transformed by it—a living crystal, vibrating and transmuting continually.

The following practices are taken from decades of teaching light meditations, and represent stages along the bridge to spiritual awakening—an aid to shifting from the personal perspective to the Divine point of view. These will especially help if you are going through the dark night of the soul, as it is light that shows the way out of despair.

When sitting in meditation, begin by closing your eyes, then imagining that you are staring into a light that floods your whole being with brightness. Instead of shielding your eyes, enjoy being blinded by this blaze, as well as the ecstasy of communion that this concentration stirs: somehow, this light triggers off memories of having been a being of pure light prior to your incarnation into your body. It stirs a recollection deep in your unconscious of moving about in a world of light, of being only light, before that formless luminosity condensed into a physical body.

Rhythmically coordinate your breath with absorbing and radiating light from the surrounding environment. Beginning with the inhalation, feel as if every pore in your body is sensitive to the light penetrating the very cells of the body—just as when you are sunbathing, for example, you feel totally receptive to the sunlight flooding your body with the warm magnetism of the sun's radiation. Or, as I like to do, you could picture yourself outside beneath the night sky, breathing in the light of the stars of far-distant galaxies. Our bodies have the capacity to absorb this gift of the light of the Universe.

Next, holding the breath between inhaling and exhaling, draw your attention to the effervescence lighting up the cells of your body in a dance of joy and delight. They begin to sparkle in communication with each other, as though exulting in the ecstasy of illumination. From the perspective of physics, what happens is that the electrons of our body cells are using the energy of light (because light is energy) to free themselves from the constraint of their orbitals. Thus, it seems that even the cells of your body have a nostalgia for freedom, the feeling of liberation that results from enlightenment. This is Jelaluddin Rumi's dance of the atoms, as well as Shiva's cosmic dance. It is an ecstatic experience of the physical phenomenon of light energizing the fabric of your body.

Then, on the exhalation, the electrons of the cells fall back into place. What remains of this dance is a glow emanating from the body. As you exhale light on the current of the breath, become conscious of radiating light outward. The more conscious you are of radiating light, the more light you radiate. Photons of light travel through space at a speed of 186,000 miles per second. This means the light you radiate reaches the stars! Since, according to physics, light is matter, the luminosity you exhale on the breath extends into space, commingling with the stars. Such an experience shatters your earthly perspective, as you realize that the light of your aura is the light of stars, which when you observed it, you thought was different from you. Indeed, your aura is just this light that has converged into a vortex—a whirlpool of light.

In fact, as you continue with this concentration, inhaling, holding, then exhaling light on the breath, you can feel the aura of light surrounding your body ebb and flow. As you inhale, feel your aura as it converges and contracts like a cosmic whirlpool in which the swirling waters of starlight accumulate toward the axis. Then, holding your breath, turn your focus deeper and deeper within, entering the void at the center of this vortex, where, like the springhead at the underground source of a lake, there is a fountain of renewal, re-energizing the cells of your body. Thus not only is your aura impacted by the convergence of the light of the stars, but by an inner luminosity as well—like the white holes in space that give birth to new stars. This way, you are not just reflecting back the light of the stars but sending out to the Cosmos a new light! Continuing this concentration on the exhalation, radiate that light through the aura back out again into the surrounding environment, imagining a scintillating interplay of rainbow colors extending out into the vast reaches of the Cosmos—a star among stars.

REMEMBERING THE WORLDS OF LIGHT

∞

The illumined dimension of human nature has been eclipsed by contemporary humankind's narrow vision of reality. Stripped of the memory of the hierarchies of light from which we originated, we are bereft of the memory of that other dimension—our true home. We have lost, as well, the luminous insight that derives from seeing life through the "eyes of God"—the Divine Glance that penetrates the secret of the mystery of life. Thus like orphans denied knowledge of their birthright, most people remain ignorant of the transcendent dimension of their being. Sundered from a sense of their heavenly inheritance, they suffer despair and limitation.

How can we break the chain of our way of thinking, re-establishing our link to the heavenly hierarchies of beings of light? How can we reconnect with our celestial counterpart—the soul of light from whose wisdom we have become separated? The answer lies in contemplating the miracle of the phenomenon of light itself. As when entering a magnificent cathedral lit by the soft glow of candles and golden rays of sunlight pouring through stained-glass windows, it is only through an encounter with something awe-inspiringly magnificent that the memory of our true nature is stirred awake. In this quest, it is light itself that is both the guide and pathway back to the pure realms of celestial spheres from which we mistakenly believe we have been exiled.

The first step in reclaiming our Divine heritage is to question those conventional conceptions of reality that close our eyes to the luminosity interlacing all of creation.

That each of us has a subtle body woven of the fabric of light is no whimsical fantasy or illusory trick of the mind. Laboratory experiments over the last decades of this century have proven that body cells absorb and re-emit light in a sparkling dance. Likewise, the famed Kirlian photographic experiments have captured on film the magnetic glow surrounding physical objects, showing how our bodies emanate a shimmering corona. Thus modern science is beginning to verify what Sufi mystics down through the centuries have taught: that the material world is a veil over a shimmering field of energy that, like a cosmic ocean of light, pervades the Universe (for light is energy). Even the sky that we may think of as empty darkness scattered here and there with stars is instead a veritable symphony of light. Astrophysicists point out that every bit of space is irradiated with the effulgence of neutrinos and cosmic rays well beyond the range of normal vision. But it is a mistake to think that the panorama of light at play throughout the Universe is "up there" in a far-distant realm. Rather, from the photons of a beer can in a gutter to the transfigured glance of a person hovering between life and death, light suffuses every level of physical, emotional, mental, and spiritual existence.

Can you imagine what life would be like if we were able to recover the memory of those lost worlds of light from which we have been exiled—cast by our own perceptual blindness into a land of shadows? Indeed, the soul drama of forgetting, then remembering, one's luminous Divinity is archetypally mythic to the human condition. This was symbolically re-enacted in the ancient Greek Eleusinian mysteries. Choirs of neophytes, or those who had not yet been initiated, donned white robes and wings that were then stripped away from them. Led by priests into the depths of a cave, they gradually began to forget the angelic choir they had once belonged to. People told them the sun is shining, the sky is blue, and the grass is green. Bereft of their memories, they could not believe that such a world had ever existed. They had come to believe that existence was nothing but dreary shadows flickering on the cave walls. Then, administering drugs that caused them to remember, priests would lead them out of captivity, bringing them once again into the blinding brilliance of daylight. This experience was a vivid re-creation of the awakening that occurs when one finds oneself once again in a forgotten world of light.

In fact, this act of remembrance is exactly the goal of the Sufism taught by Hazrat Inayat Khan. Incidentally, when someone is initiated, we say, "May you find the path that leads you toward the purpose of your life, illumination."

Thus as ours is a way of light, the work we do as followers of the path of Sufism is to help others become conscious that they are beings of light. Just like a potter works with clay to shape a pot, work with light practices helps individuals become more luminous and radiant. Becoming more skilled in the art of illumination catalyzes transformation. How would the world be different if, for example, all of us were to reclaim our inheritance as members in a "tribe of light" who vow to bring enlightenment to all creation? If more and more people were to infuse the consciousness of light into their interactions—their intimate relationships, their work, and physical activities—the healing effect on others would be immeasurable. Just contemplating the idea of light during conversation has an instantaneous effect, as it awakens within another his own nature as a being of light. Even if that person is materialistic, or filled with anger, steadfastly maintaining the light in one's own soul reinforces the light within him as well. As soon as we encounter another person who is filled with light, his presence acts as a torch sparking our own light.

How vividly I recall, for instance, looking for a *rishi* in a cave above Rishikesh in India. I was with a group of people who suddenly exclaimed, "There he is, up there!" When I looked up the hill in the direction they were pointing, all I could see was an enormous white light. Peering more closely, I dimly discerned the outline of a man in the midst of a beautiful white aura. Just being in his presence was so illuminating, so beautiful, and so inspiring. In the same way, I recall a group of young people who went to visit a Catholic monastery in the Algerian desert. They spent the entire duration of their stay meditating on light—when they emerged from seclusion they were visibly sparkling and radiant. So enchanted, so wonderful is it to meditate on light

that most of my own practices are spent simply working with light.

As these examples of my own experiences and those
of others show, there is a direct connection between
illumination and awakening. The beauty of the word
illumination, or enlightenment, is that it is referring to
light as a concrete term for awakening. This is because
meditating on light triggers an altered state of awareness that takes us to a level of being that we had forgotten. Likewise, the more awake one is, the more light
one radiates in one's glance and in one's aura. So awakening triggers illumination and vice versa—producing
a radiance in the aura and in one's countenance, as well
as clarity of thought. In this way, light offers a tangible launching platform for consciousness, bridging the
worlds of matter and spirit. The path of illumination
proceeds on that bridge of light by means of specific
meditation practices that offset consciousness in the
same way a photographer adjusts the lens on his camera. As we proceed further along this bridge of light,
we shift gradually from the personal pole of our being
to the cosmic dimension of consciousness, finally stepping off the bridge into the ocean of the light of Divine
intelligence—the crowning moment of awakening.

Now, let your imagination have free rein in representing to yourself the most incredible skyscapes of
light and color: explosions of sunbursts, sunrises, and
sunsets; radiant fountains of diaphanous waterdrops;
soft-lit moonscapes; gloriously fiery lightning storms;

and waves of colors fanning out into a jewel-toned rainbow like a peacock spreading its tail across the turquoise sky.

This reverie on landscapes of light can be followed by casting one's consciousness out into the sparkling, starry sky. Shifting your perspective from its vantage point on planet earth into outer space, extend the reach of your vision into far-distant galactic regions. Imagine that you yourself are a being of light hurtling into the ocean of sheer radiance that is the Cosmos. Lifted above the tribulations and limitations of everyday existence, you find that you can fly wherever your heart takes you, carried aloft on wings of ecstasy. Floating among these sublime skyscapes of light, you find that your consciousness expands in an ever-widening embrace of the Cosmos. One could imagine a hierarchy of beings of light behind all material existence. Suddenly the planets, molecules, atoms, electrons, and galaxies are revealed as a multitude of spiritual beings.

Awakening to the fact that there is no inanimate matter, you may also be startled by the way in which your attunement mirrors the hidden forms of the Universe. The opposite is also true: your attunement will help you grasp something you had never envisioned before. For example, you might notice clusters of light fragmenting into sparks, which would corroborate your sense of unique individuality. Or, you may experience the serenity of a peaceful sunset, reflecting the serenity of unity. You might even witness a battle taking place in the Universe: volcanic eruptions and fire gushing forth from the conflicts of opposing forces. During the course of your meditation, you may choose to engage in this battle as a knight of light, rather than becoming a victim of violence. There may, as well, be encounters with obedient light beings, as well as rebellious light beings that hurtle through space unpredictably like comets—reflecting your intense need for freedom. Gradually, you realize that this vast Cosmos of light reflects the drama of your own life, as well as the struggle within your being to uphold the values you hold most dear.

LUCIFERIAN LIGHT VS. TRUE ILLUMINATION: POLISHING THE MIRROR OF THE HEART

∞

As many teachers before have proclaimed, there is an ongoing battle in the Universe—between the pure light of selfless dedication to the highest ideal, and Luciferian light that is clouded with the shadows of selfish egotism. What exactly is Luciferian light? It is light that has become disconnected from its Divine source. When we lose our sense of belonging to the totality, our experience of light can become misleading, deceptive, and ultimately counterproductive, as in the case of Lucifer, the fallen angel. This acts as a warning to those, for example, who want to work with the aura in order to become more personally radiant, rather than seeing the self within the context of the Divine light of the whole Universe.

In fact, before undertaking practices with light, it is important to recognize that there are moral issues surrounding enlightenment that must be confronted. Reactions such as greed, intolerance, impatience, resentment, anger, or cruelty block the process of deep transformation, locking us into our separateness. If these shadows are present, a person may be able to attain a certain state of luminosity, but it will be Luciferian light that can be used for the wrong purposes—whether manipulation, intrigue, or personal gain. Thus if we want to fulfill our deep longing for light, we need to look within to see what it is that veils the light of the Universe. This is the shadow described by Jung—the light of our being is always present, undefiled and pure as a child, but it is hidden unless we are able to meticulously work with each of those elements beclouding the light. Then negative emotions can be transmuted into positive, powerful feelings of love, compassion, and generosity. Light practices require a capacity for profound truthfulness—a process that can be facilitated by psychological self-examination.

ENCOUNTERING YOUR
CELESTIAL COUNTERPART

∽

As you begin to shift away from your skinbound identity to your aura, you begin to sense that your aura is
the template in which your magnetic field is formed.
In fact, your magnetic field is the template in which
your body is being formed. Thus your aura is config-
ured in a shape. It is a real body fashioned in the fabric
of light; but though it follows the contours of your
physical body, it does not have a profile and is more like
the corona of radiance surrounding the petals of flowers. It doesn't have the consistency of matter; it changes
continually, reflecting your thinking and attunement.
It glows particularly strongly in your acts of glorification.

As Ibn 'Arabi says, all faces are His Face. You could
say that the Divine Face is trying to manifest through
your face. It is often the case during meditations on
light that the form of a face suddenly appears. This may
sound theoretical. But the simple story of a mother who
shows her child one of those pictures that contain hidden forms within them illustrates the state of consciousness I am trying to illustrate. The child looks and
looks, unable to pinpoint the shape of a fairy in a tree,
when suddenly she sees it and her whole face lights up
with awareness as she exclaims, "Yes, I see the fairy in
the tree!" In other words, the light of intelligence

affects the light of the body and its aura. That is why the two words, awakening and illumination, are interconnected. There is a direct relationship between this clear light of awareness, or illumination, and what we call awakening.

A Gnostic text describes a vision in which a sage was walking in a landscape of light; surrounding him were forms that he couldn't quite make out. Then, just off in the mist, the form of a magnificent face seemed to emerge. Gradually assuming a whole form, it then seemed as though a person was approaching him, while at the same time he was walking toward that person. At first, he was overwhelmed by the splendor that was coming through, when suddenly it struck him that the being resembled himself. Finally, in a moment of sublime illumination, he realized that the being facing him was his soul, his celestial counterpart.

The sage's description of this mystical communion with his celestial counterpart illustrates the way in which, at first glance, one's real self can appear in such glorious raiment that we assume it is a being separate from ourselves. Especially if we have a negative self-image, it is difficult to identify with our spiritual counterpart. Our self-image is typically based on the limited concept we have of ourselves as no more than our body and the worldly persona we have fashioned in order to survive. And because we have had to develop certain aspects of ourselves in order to survive the battle of life, we think of ourselves as irrevocably defiled.

Yet in truth, our self-image is nothing in comparison to what we really are. Our original, celestial nature is immaculate, genuine, and completely lacking in any guile or artifice. Therefore what we need to be reminded of is that just as the voice of the singer Caruso has been retrieved by modern-day technicians from the distortion of old recordings, so, too, is it possible to recover the memory of our true self. For while our earthly face could be said to be a distortion of our celestial counterpart—the core of our being unconcerned with adapting itself to the environment—the recollection of the heavenly state is so powerful it will transfigure our aura, causing it to flower into great beauty. Just realizing this can make all the difference; it is knowledge that can transform our bodies, give energy in old age, joy in suffering, and insight into the guile of people. That is why the Tibetans speak of spiritual realization as the "pure light of bliss": awakening to one's true nature restores wholeness and happiness.

CHAKRAS:
THE JACOB'S LADDER
OF LIGHT
∞

Light could be considered the ladder that raises the soul toward its highest ideal. The force that propels us upward on this ladder of realization, however, is what

Hazrat Inayat Khan calls a "passion for the unattainable": the intense feelings of ecstasy that result from our discovery of our celestial counterpart, and an overwhelming nostalgia to glimpse further visions of the heavenly spheres. Like the fuel that launches a rocket, these emotions help raise our consciousness from one level to another.

While thus far we have worked with the principle of fluorescence—absorbing visible light from nature and the starry Cosmos—there is a different principle called phosphorescence, or the ability of the body itself to produce light. This is the metaphysical skill by which we learn to transmute infrared light into visible light and even ultraviolet light. It is a function found in nature, from fireflies that emit light, to those animals that don't have access to sunlight, such as bats in caves, and certain species of deep-sea fish. In the same way, Hazrat Inayat Khan taught that meditation allows us to develop faculties that have tremendous potential to open the doors of perception to new levels of consciousness.

The secret of ascending the Jacob's ladder of light to further planes of realization is that of concentrating on the *chakras* and their corresponding spectrum of colors. This is captured in the image of a flame rising up a chimney. If you have ever observed a flame closely, for example, you will have noticed that the base is red, and it then shifts subtly across a spectrum of colors from carmine, orange, gold, yellow, green, blue, violet, and ultimately, ultraviolet. To do this practice in synchrony with the breath, begin by exhaling as long a breath as you are physically capable of. This will enable you to inhale longer, maintaining your concentration on each *chakra*.

So, after a lengthy exhalation, breathe in deeply, imagining that a flame is rising inside you along your spinal cord. The very bottom of your spine glows bright red; then, the second *chakra*, or reproductive center, shades into a terra cotta color, something like the color of the robes of the Hindu *sannyasins*. The third *chakra*, or solar plexus, flames a bright orange like the clouds that you see at dawn or sunset. In the fourth *chakra*, or heart center, the flame burns royally golden, then shifts to a deep emerald green in the fifth *chakra*, or throat center.

Next, transfer your attention to the radiance of your eyes, and in addition your third eye. The color we perceive is an indication of the frequency of light waves. The frequency of this light of the eyes is sky blue, and the third eye, violet, is located at the center of the forehead just above and between the eyes. This *chakra* is associated with the pineal gland—a gland responsive to the light radiating from the center of the galaxy that, in my view, links us to the evolutionary thrust of the Universe.

Now, raise your consciousness to the crown center at the top of the head, turning the focalized spotlight of the third eye upward and out through the crown in a radiant arabesque of scintillating ultraviolet light, spraying streams and droplets of light like a water fountain. This is also the location of the pituitary gland; it can be physically stimulated by holding one's breath, then pressing the tip of one's tongue up against the roof of the mouth and turning the eyeballs upward. This has the effect of awakening the whole endocrine system. Consequently, the subtle chemistry of your body is now serving as a support system for your realization—transforming the denser cells of your body into those finer cells that are the neurotransmitters, enzymes, and hormones of the autonomic nervous system. In this way, both the physical and subtle bodies have become transformed into a ladder, or support system, for attaining spiritual realization.

THE LIGHT THAT CAN BE SEEN AND THE LIGHT THAT SEES

∞

Beyond the visible world lie different levels of light. Indeed, concentration on the *chakras* is a technique by which we learn to transmute visible light into invisible light, crossing the bridge into the zones that lie beyond the celestial realms. The heart center, for instance, is connected with a radiant aureole of light that extends outward heightened by generosity—much like the familiar picture of Christ with his heart illuminated from within and emitting a warm, lantern-like glow. The throat *chakra* is a vibrational level of consciousness that regulates your "audio body," through which you can attune to your unique "signature note." The third eye brings us into contact with very high levels of light, which could be described as the heavenly spheres.

At this stage, we pass from visibly radiant light to what the Sufis call the light of intelligence. Indeed, the Sufis make a clear distinction between the light that can be seen and the light that sees. The light that can be seen is powerfully radiant. It is light that is focalized into form, whether a shining star, a many-hued rainbow, or the magnetic shimmer of the subtle body's aura. Invisible light, however, does not radiate from a point in space. Rather, it is a diffuse luminosity coming from within, what Hazrat Inayat Khan refers to as the "all-pervading light" suffusing the Cosmos. One could say that it is the uncreated light, the Divine energy, from which creation is shaped.

So it is at this stage in your meditation that you make the quantum leap beyond the level of form and existence to that of pure realization. Thus, on the inhalation of the breath, let your consciousness flame upward along the pathway of the *chakras*, experiencing your body's transmutation into light. It is important to remember that your body is multi-tiered and exists at several levels: the physical body, the subtle body, and aura are each more subtle than the others. Thus as your aura and subtle body intensify the light frequency, so, too, does the physical body change. Likewise, there is an impact of our magnetic force field upon the structure of our body cells. What has been held to be resurrection may be accounted for by the fact that the electrons of our body cells are gradually transformed into photons—just the way flowers transform themselves into the quintessence of perfume as their petals decay.

Next, hold the breath, but now, instead of concentrating on the rainbow above your head as in the previous concentration, meditate on the clear light of intelligence that is beyond time, space, and existence. Whereas before you were visualizing radiant light— ranging from the stars in the sky to the light of the *chakras* in your body—at this stage you lay aside any notion of matter, subtle matter, and aura, immersing yourself in a state of formless awareness beyond imagination. Here your mind stretches beyond its individual boundaries to encompass the thinking of the Universe. It is a state where you recover the experiences of levels where consciousness is absorbed into its ground, which is intelligence. Sufis call this unveiling the light of Divine Intelligence that has been covered over by veils of illusion. It corresponds with the last words of Buddha, "I have overcome determinism." In other words, it is the ultimate, absolute freedom from all things that have locked you into a rut—your thinking, self-image, actions, opinions, separateness—and that block seeing your participation with the totality of the Universe. Suddenly, you have a feeling of awakening, like the flash of lightning the Tibetans call *vajra*, or what Christian mystics describe as the quickening of the Holy Spirit. (At this stage, the meditator may pause, relaxing the breath in this state of enlightened consciousness.)

AWAKENING IN LIFE
∞

As transcendently blissful and peaceful as the state of *samadhi* may be, however, awakening beyond life can never be the final goal of spiritual practice. It has to be followed by awakening in life. This means seeing life through the eyes of God—the Universe—casting the light of your realization upon the intractable problems and emotional sufferings of a human being on planet earth. By realization, I mean the knowledge and innate wisdom that is already written into what is called your soul but which has been obscured by your reliance on circumstances in the outer world. It is the difference between what the Sufis describe as acquired knowledge and revealed knowledge.

So, to continue with the previous concentration— inhaling up along the *chakras*, then holding the breath, suspended in a state of pure intelligence and all-pervading awareness—exhale out through your eyes the light of realization you experienced in these states of higher consciousness. Poetically captured in the phrase from the Qur'an, a "light upon a light," the experience of casting the light of the Divine through the beams of the glance radically transforms your previous perspective. Whereas before you may have seen only meaninglessness and unnecessary suffering in life's chaos and confusion, now you are able to grasp the underlying purposefulness that has thus far eluded you. At first, this experience confers upon your consciousness a grand overview, like flying in a helicopter over a city. Those dervishes observing life from this height say that God has granted each human being a measure of his own freedom, at the risk of the misuse of this freedom. Yet you also perceive the intention behind circumstances going awry: the Universe is dynamic and evolving, rather than a "puppet show" where all events are predetermined. From this perspective, it becomes apparent that it is by learning through countless mistakes and wrong turns that individuals fulfill the Divine purpose for which they were born, thereby contributing to the ever-evolving destiny of all humankind.

Thus as you cast your intelligence through your glance, you penetrate deeply into the nature of this mystery. It is as if there were a lot of puzzle pieces strewn about—and suddenly things fall into place. It is through the insight conferred upon you by your spiritual realization that you are able to see the difference between those relationships and activities in everyday life that bring you in harmony with the Universe, and those things that cause you to fall out of step. And that is why it is so important to bring those insights gained from awakening beyond life into everyday life. The best analogy I can offer for the process of awakening in life is to imagine that you have gone to see a magnificent piece of architecture, a marvelous building that is absolutely enchanting. Then, you visit the architect who drew up the plans for this building and therefore knew exactly what he had in mind for its purpose. Imagine that this architect shows you his drawings, and then takes you on a tour of the building, explaining why the building was constructed the way that it was. That is what I mean by awakening in life: seeing the programming, the intent, that the Universe had in mind.

Working with the third eye can help you to overcome the powerful pull of the conditioning of the surrounding environment. In addition, however, your spiritual insight can be strengthened through concentrations involving the third eye. Before beginning this technique, it is important to remember that you should never work with the third eye as a way of projecting or intensifying your personal gaze to influence, hypnotize, or exercise power over people. One way to guard against this pitfall is to observe the sacredness of your glance so that it may in no way be inquisitive or personal. One may use one's third eye only if one's glance has become totally purified, as if bathed in heavenly light.

Think of your eyes as the headlights of a car. As you

exhale, project these beams forward into the darkness, concentrating on the laserlike beam that descends through the crown center like a shaft of light. The light of the third eye may be threaded through the beams of the physical eye. Now, as you inhale, turn your eyeballs upward. Concentrate upon a fountain of light rising toward the top of the head. As you hold your breath you could try to enter into the consciousness of celestial beings and think that the planets and the stars that we perceive are the bodies of these beings. You could even choose one in particular, such as the sun of our solar system. Piercing through its outer glory that manifests in sunrises and sunsets, enter directly into the consciousness of the nonphysical being of the sun. Then, stepping through the consciousness of this regal being, you ascend into the consciousness of even more cosmic beings, each one a fragment of the group which is hierarchically above them.

Now, slowly exhale once more, bringing all that light down through your glance and out through the third eye, knowing that your glance is like an extension of the light that sees, instead of the light that can be seen—the light of the hierarchies of pure, luminous intelligences, manifesting what the Sufis call the *Nur-al-anwar*, the light of lights. Linking your glance with this light is the secret of looking into the souls of people. It is not Luciferian, but heavenly, and impersonal—what the Sufis call generous, loving light, untainted by selfishness. Unconditional love which is inspired by Divine Love does not brook either personal power or any kind of resentment, just pure, giving light. Your sincerity will manifest through your glance and communicate to other beings.

COMMUNING WITH LIGHT: *SAMADHI* WITH OPEN EYES

∞

"He is the seer and also that through which He sees."

— IBN 'ARABI

◆

Now, rather than focusing on the objects in front of you, keep your eyes aimed at infinity; this causes anything in your line of vision to fall out of focus and appear as a blur, as if everything were intermeshed with everything else. You can also open and close your eyes rapidly, like a shutter in a camera. In this practice you don't "see" as you normally would, but cast light forward into the physical realm, imagining your eyes and your body as extensions of the Universe.

Then think to yourself, "My glance is the Divine Glance. It has been greatly limited by my perspectives—but it is the Divine Glance radiating luminous intelligence." As you exhale imagine that the eyes of God are scanning the horizon. As you inhale, imagine that you are in a state of awaiting, rather than actively looking. When I was in the Royal Navy during World War II, I spent four hours every night watching for German U-boats. I was taught then that my eyesight had to be totally neutral and receptive. The same technique can be applied here. Think of the Divine Glance as having a penetrating effect. The Sufis call it the light of intelligence that sees into the nature of things. With diligent and insistent practice, you will begin to grasp a kind of halo around objects in your environment. Take, for example, a flower. Instead of looking at each petal, gaze at the flower as a whole, entering into its spirit. Eventually you see its aura, sensing the reality that lies just behind its physical representation as a single blossom. Or, you can do this practice with a person, glimpsing the luminescent countenance of his celestial counterpart transpiring through the features of his face. The poet Hafiz says, "If only you could see yourself through my eyes, you'd realize how beautiful you are." That is the privilege I have often as a teacher, watching the faces of those I am guiding in meditation.

Indeed, this is an esoteric practice that can be used in a tangible way to commune more deeply with life, nature, and people. Suppose, for example, that you are walking through a lovely, green forest in a state of ecstasy, thinking, "Yes, my eyes are the eyes through which God sees. They are the eyes through which God sees His own body." Such a perspective awakens an entirely new dimension that facilitates a more mystical participation with nature, rather than that of the detached human "observer." This was the experience of

St. Francis, who, rather than merely observing the leaves and trunks of the trees when walking through the forest, entered into the very consciousness of the trees. It was what led him to proclaim, "That which you are looking for is looking at you." Further, you realize that your glance is the Divine Glance, yet greatly diminished.

Such a state of consciousness is not *samadhi* with closed eyes—it is being awake in life with open eyes. It is seeing mind in matter; it is grasping meaningfulness even in the midst of our everyday exchanges with others that the ordinary mind couldn't see. The penetrating light of one's glance, for instance, can cut through the false exterior of the *persona,* penetrating people's souls and revealing their deepest motivations and attunement. The light of Divine Intelligence is not just cognitive, however, but creative, unfurling people's highest potentials. This kind of exchange can take place in the most ordinary of circumstances. Say, for example, that you're sitting in a room with someone, talking. You may be exchanging thoughts, as well as deep feelings. But at the same time, you can also commune in each other's light.

You do this by first becoming aware of a person's aura. Rather than focusing on a person's tangible features, for instance—the color of his eyes, or the contours of his mouth and nose—you take more notice of his subtle expression, commingling the light in your eyes with the light in his eyes. Perhaps the person doesn't realize what you are doing; yet, because you're honoring his higher nature, it helps him to feel comfortable with himself. Basking in the light of your aura, his real being is given permission to shine through. For just as a firefly brightens the night with its warm glow, so, too, can we bring light to others, irradiating them with our aura.

One of the more advanced light practices involves visualizing your aura as a container into which you invite people. Within this radiant circumference, you can imagine embracing them with light and, in the process, healing and transforming them by integrating them into your meditation on light. If you are visiting patients in a hospital, simply commiserating with their suffering does not really alleviate their pain. Likewise, neither does an attitude of casual flippancy. Yet you can help bring healing to someone who is ill or depressed simply by the light that flashes through your glance when you smile.

THE SMILING FOREHEAD
∞

This silent ability to impart to others the light of Divine Intelligence, and all its attendant qualities of joy, warmth, insight, and revelation, is captured in a Sufi phrase, "the smiling forehead." For illumination is always linked with a kind of smile, like the mysterious, lingering smile of the Buddha. I remember visiting a museum in San Francisco, for example, where I saw a little statue of a Chinese monk. The monk's facial expression conveyed how absolutely carried away he was by the ecstasy of awakening. Who knows what his real-life story was; no doubt he had experienced a lot of pain and sadness. But through light he had overcome human limitation, transmuting his suffering into a smile of Divine Bliss.

The secret contained within the mystical expression of the smiling forehead is that it is possible to be both joyful and sad at the same time. For while it's very difficult to feel happy when there is so much suffering in the world, one's soul needs to smile. And though suffering can never be overcome by joy, it is possible to conjoin the two together. This is done by encompassing the whole spectrum of our nature, in both its human and Divine dimensions. At one end of our being, for example, we are individuals with all the limitations of the human condition. At the other end, however, our beings are coextensive with the Universe. At some level we are beings of light among the hierarchies of luminous spirits of intelligence. The saving grace of our higher being can be filtered down into the personal dimension. Thus no matter how badly things go in life, we can still smile, because we have transmuted the emotions of both suffering and joy into ecstasy—that mystical state out of which the Cosmos was born.

That is the intent of meditating with light: to restore you to your original nature as a majestic being of light. Reconnected to your real self, you see things as that monk saw them. You feel illuminated from within by radiant joy, as though the very cells of your body are dancing with the ecstasy of Divine knowledge. You are smiling, but it's not your cheeks that are smiling; it's your forehead that is aglow with the reflected glory of the celestial spheres from which you are descended. Now your thinking is crystal clear, sparkling, with no trace of ambiguity, compromise, or mental dishonesty. Your understanding is the Divine Understanding; your intelligence, even the very constitution of your brain, is of the same nature as the Cosmos. As Newton said, you think as God thinks.

FIVE

AWAKENING IN LIFE:

HOW OUR PERSONAL PROBLEMS CAN BECOME THE CATALYSTS FOR SPIRITUAL CREATIVITY

"The fulfillment of the Divine purpose is to be found in the human being who is God-conscious."

— HAZRAT INAYAT KHAN

❖

Can you imagine how your problems might look from God's point of view, or envision how God might resolve them? Do you ever ask yourself what is the reason for the circumstances of your life? Have you ever considered the notion that those vexing dilemmas that plague your daily life are challenging you to open to new ways of thinking? Can you sense how these difficulties are the means through which something mysterious, perhaps even great, is struggling to be born through you?

Thus far our meditations have borne us aloft toward the peaks of spiritual transcendence, where we have been granted a magnificent overview of all creation and insight into the mysteries of life. Now it is time to concentrate this overview upon the ordinary realm of everyday life. For, as I have pointed out, awakening beyond life must be followed by awakening in life. At this level of realization, you are able to cast the light of the intelligence of the Universe upon your problems instead of judging things the way they appear from your personal point of view.

This descent is called *tanzil* in Sufism, or the way in which the Divine Thinking expresses itself in the phenomenal world. By applying the expanded and detached perspective we have gained in our previous meditations to our day-to-day circumstances, the problems that once seemed insurmountable now appear in an entirely different light. In fact, everything may seem quite the opposite of how it once appeared. Just like the accounts of astronauts who return to earth transformed by their vision of the planet earth from outer space, so, too, from the vantage point of altered states of consciousness do we suddenly see the experience of human life as so precious, rare, and poignant that we feel ashamed for having let ourselves be consumed by petty grudges and fleeting temptations. From the viewpoint of our higher self, it's like having been invited to the Divine Banquet—only to pick up crumbs from the floor.

In fact, one reason many of us have difficulty reconciling the spiritual dimension with the wordly stems from the misguided notion that the drama of life itself—the frustrations of earning a living, the suffering caused by ill health or the emotional roller coaster of intimate relationships—make it difficult to attain, or sustain, illumination. Yet it's just in the midst of such difficult situations that one can find illumination. Rather than prevent unfoldment, such stresses challenge us to develop heroism. Instead of permanent roadblocks on the spiritual path, the obstacles we face are creative catalysts for spiritual evolution. What had seemed a defeat avers itself in our new realization to be a victory. For as wonderful as meditation is, the true test of spiritual realization lies in how well we manage to deal with our day, and whether or not there is a difference in how we handle our problems.

Often, the tendency is to slip back into the same state of mind we were in before our meditation. Even after having had the breakthrough that enabled us to see how uninspiring and inadequate our old strategies proved to be, the habits by which we handled our day-to-day circumstances die hard. Thus the task is to learn to build a bridge between altered states of consciousness and our real-life situations in the outer world. For myself, I find that when faced with the onrush of urgent, compelling activities, it helps to keep in mind the deeper reality that lies concealed by overt appearances. In order to prevent overlooking my dedication to fulfilling higher ideals in order to meet my day-to-day commitments, I continuously ask myself, "What are you doing in life? Have you forgotten what it is all about?" Even more important, I question what is really at stake behind the drama that is being enacted.

In fact, according to the teachings of the ancient Sufis, what is at stake is giving birth to the Universe's unborn qualities. Like Divine genes that are latent within the psyche, attributes such as compassion, mercy, truth, power, forgiveness, and many other qualities are the fruits born of life's stuggles. The crucible within which this alchemical process occurs is the arena of everyday decision making and problem solving: to marry this person or remain single; to speak the truth or remain silent; to keep faith with one's soul destiny or settle for a comfortable lifestyle; to protect the environment from degradation or turn one's head away.

Those difficult situations that we struggle to be free of are in reality the birth pangs through which God is being born in everyday life; and the means through which our soul evolves. From this vantage point, meditation is less a means of retreating from life in order to awaken into higher states of consciousness, and becomes instead a rehearsal for life itself. It is a method of changing one's perspective in order to effect a change in one's circumstances. Even if a particular situation doesn't change, the resulting shift in perspective can allow us to see how something that had once filled us with despair is somehow exactly right because it is providing a difficult, but valuable, spiritual lesson.

This lesson always has to do with the unfolding of new patterns and ways of being. In the birth of a child, for instance, one could say that the Universe is re-creating itself in an entirely new way. This rebirthing process can also manifest in us in a new psychological and spiritual pattern. Buddhist teachings point out that human beings become trapped in the vicious cycle of illusion, repeating lifetime after lifetime on the *samsaric* wheel. A person does what everyone else does: grows up, gets married, has children, works, gets ill, grows old, and dies. In this manner, life goes on and on without making much sense. Nothing is gained.

But now suppose that we evolve in a way that the *samsaric* wheel doesn't just keep turning on its axis — but advances forward. In order for it to advance, however, it has to be pulled forward by something greater than itself. What this means is that whatever those deeply embedded habits and conditions are that prevent us from changing — whether our ancestral, educational, or cultural upbringing — they can be overcome only through a vision of how one "could be if one would be as one might be." That's spiritual creativity — seeing how the problems in our lives can be re-framed as catalysts for Divine artistry. For while Sufis and Buddhists both employ teachings of detachment and self-transcendence, Sufis believe neither that the body and mind are just the products of our ancestors, nor that we are the victims of a mysterious process that happened against our will, but that there is a quality within us that is uniquely purposeful and useful within the overall plan of the Universe.

In *samadhi*, for example, the focus is not so much on

responsibility, but on otherworldliness. In Sufism, however, an initiate is considered a vice-regent of God who takes responsibility for the human condition. Rather than leave the world behind, the Sufi surveys the realm of his or her personal domain, saying, in effect, "I was so involved in my own personal problems, or trying to be entertained by life, that I forgot that there are others who need me." This might, for example, result in my writing a letter to someone, or answering a letter rather than ignoring it. Surveying one's "kingdom" or "queendom" with an eye to those qualities life is seeking to bring forth can result in a sense of responsibility that conveys authority and sovereignty, and fosters the flowering of one's personality.

Thus from the Sufi standpoint the spiritual journey is about much more than detaching from the illusory conditions of life; it is creative and transformative. In the old days, in Morocco or Afghanistan, for example, a person could go to the bazaar and see skilled artisans making beautiful trays, carpets, pottery, and clothes. It is no different with our personality: our personalities are like lumps of clay, loose threads, or bolts of cloth that, through the formative influence of the problems and challenges we face in life, are refashioned into exquisite expressions of the marvelous bazaar of Divine Qualities. The only difference is that, unlike artists' raw materials, the bounty of God's perfection cannot manifest as reality without our conscious participation. As Hazrat Inayat Khan said, "God can entertain a greater degree of perfection in a being who participates in his creativity." Indeed, the ultimate work of art is ourselves, our personality. We are each endowed with the faculty of being able to become what we want to become; life is a great loss if we don't avail ourselves of this potential. So remember: How we could be is so much greater than the way we've become. The future lies before us; we create it through our imagination in the same way that the whole Universe is created by the Divine Imagination.

QUESTIONING YOUR ASSUMPTIONS: WHAT IF?

∞

The first step in releasing the creative potential contained within your everyday problems is to question your assumptions: Indeed, your problems are not what you think they are. The practice of inquiring more deeply into thought patterns is reflected in most esoteric traditions. According to the Hindu tradition of Yoga, for example, the physical world is not as it appears; neither is the psyche. Both are formed of *maya*, or the slippery stuff of illusion. This timeless insight corresponds with the discoveries of modern-day physicists who now know that matter is not the tangible, solid substance we think it is but a paradoxical network beyond our understanding that looks different to different points of view.

The same thing is true of your problems. Those issues that you face are not fixed in time and space; they are relative to your particular viewpoint and subject to constant change. In fact, much of the pain caused by our problems stems in part from our own unchanging biases in terms of how we interpret our personal difficulties to ourselves. To say that we are biased, however, is not to say that we are wrong. Sufism does not discount the individual viewpoint—it stresses the importance of realizing that our view is only one point of view, and that one learns to see things from various angles. For what spirituality is all about is cultivating an ever-widening perspective. Keeping ourselves jammed up in our own narrow standpoint leads to nothing more than turning around in circles like a fly in a bottle—you can't get out.

Thus in the initial phase of reflecting on your problems, the first thing to do is to downplay your assessment of your problems. Just the way you turned away from the demands of the outside world at the outset of your retreat, so, too, do you want to take the paradoxical approach of facing your problems by first stepping back from them. As this may be difficult, you might want to distract yourself by listening to a soothing piece of music, or perhaps practice some of the contemplations mentioned in chapter 3. The intent of these practices is to help you bypass the thinking of your ordinary mind—your mind can't solve your problems. It will only limit you to a certain perspective.

Once you have managed to turn your attention away

from your problem as it appears to you, then you are ready to begin practicing the skill of extending your consciousness into various other points of view. One method of doing this is by looking at your life from the point of view of another person. How might another person, for instance, perceive your problem—your elderly uncle, a psychotherapist, the neighbor down the street, or even a character from another period in history? Yet another method of extending consciousness with regard to your problems is by entering into the consciousness of another person who is looking at a problem in which you both are involved.

Often, for example, we tend to think that we are right while the other person is wrong when the case might well be that we are wrong and the other person is right. Though this may be difficult to know for sure, at least this exercise helps you to look at your problem from two vantage points, rather than just one. It helps you to understand that while you see things one way, the other party sees things differently. A third exercise in expanding consciousness is to imagine how you look from the point of view of that other person. You might discover that they have an image of you that isn't how you see yourself at all. Likewise, you might discover that your image of the other person is distorted as well, leading to two errors of miscommunication. In fact, most of us spend our entire lives making judgments based on error, allowing our misassessments of others and ourselves to muddy the waters of perception.

What these practices are leading to is the ability to

clarify the thinking process, so that life can be examined from a much deeper place. By questioning the validity of those assessments we automatically assume to be incontrovertibly right, we uncover a deeper level of thought. Like flying fish over water, most of us observe only the surface of life without grasping what's really happening underneath. This leads to hastily made conclusions. But by placing a buffer between the problem and our individual ego, we can forestall such automatic responses, drawing instead from the insights gleaned through seeing our problems through a much wider lens.

Freeing yourself from your previously narrow interpretation of your problems will give you a sense of freedom. Just imagine, all the time you thought things were a certain way—only to discover that you were wrong! Isn't that fantastic? Can you imagine—everything that you had previously thought, everything that you had been convinced of so far, was wrong! No doubt this experience might be terrifying at first—as if the rug had been pulled out from under you—but it is the first step on the path toward genuine freedom of mind. From this perspective emotionallycharged thoughts dissipate beneath your penetrating inquiry into their validity. If you don't trust your assessments of your problems, they don't have any impact on your being. In India this process of peeling away the layers of disillusion is called *neti, neti,* or "It is not this, it is not that."

Sufism, however, wants to know what is rather than

what is not. Indeed, one could say that the motto for the spirituality of the future is "What if?" What if things are not as I thought; what if they are really about something entirely different? What if I am much more than the limited self I thought I was, and what if my problems are really about the unfolding of God's potential through me?

DISCOVERING YOUR SPIRITUAL ANCESTRY

Most of us believe that our character or personality, with all its idiosyncrasies and limitations, is something that we have to live with whether we like it or not, much the same way we have accepted the body we have been given at birth. Yet to think of the personality as a mere by-product of one's history is fatalistic. In fact, I believe it is possible to completely transform our personalities not necessarily by denying our ancestry, but through discovering an extra dimension of ourselves— our spiritual heritage.

A story from the life of St. Francis helps to illustrate what I am trying to explain. At one point in his life, St. Francis was arraigned before a local judge by his father, who had a shop selling cloth and wanted his son to follow in his footsteps. But St. Francis was too busy building churches and helping the poor to work with his father. When he was brought before the judge for a hearing, his father pointed out that everything his son possessed came from him—even the clothes he wore. At that point, St. Francis took off his clothes and said, "I have another father." Through his choice of words, St. Francis acknowledged his earthly inheritance—while at the same time asserted his spiritual legacy as well.

The knowledge that we are the descendants of both our earthly parents and our Divine parents is hinted at in Christ's words "Be ye perfect as your Father." Similarly, Hazrat Inayat Khan said, "The ego is a false notion of what we are." What these statements highlight is that most of us, as we struggle through life, attempt to derive our strength solely from our self-image as a separate ego—a source of weakness that ultimately compounds our problems. Especially when faced with extremely challenging situations, there is a tendency to fall back on the ego, resorting to its inadequate strategies of defenses, denial, or wishful thinking. Only by recalling to mind the all-embracing dimension of our higher being that is the Divine Ego and that we touch upon during peak moments of meditation can we begin to overcome the counterproductive tendencies of the personal self.

I can tell you about an experience that I once had that describes the beauty and the outlook of the higher self. During a retreat that I was leading, an elderly lady went into a comatose state. She was dying and in a delirium. As I knelt down next to her, I held her hand in mine; even though she was in a coma she felt my presence. Her eyes fluttered open, and, in that moment, all her wrinkles disappeared. Before my eyes she became a young girl—radiant, full of light, and totally transfigured. My perception of her wasn't fantasy, but her true countenance transpiring through her physical face. It is our ignorance of this dimension of ourselves that causes our mishandling of situations, resulting in suffering.

Rather than wait for the crowning moment of death, however, the practical wisdom of meditation is to develop the skill of connecting to the real self now; the experience of immensity we are granted when we do so gives us enormous power and resilience to face life's challenges. Hope opens up, as by turning within we are more likely to grasp the essence of the problem, instead of being caught by the way it appears at the surface. Through this insight, we can see the connection that exists between our problems and the way we have been approaching them. And once we see that, then we can also awaken to the realization that a transformation in consciousness can lead to a breakthrough in our problems.

Creative Prayer: In this practice, you are going to take some time aside from your problems, and turn your attention within to connect, like St. Francis did, to your spiritual heritage. How is this done? In addition to reconnecting to your celestial counterpart through the light practices in the previous chapter, one of the most creative forms of prayer is that of meditating on the Divine Qualities. During the act of glorifying God through prayer, for instance, you project upon Him the qualities that you are familiar with in yourself and others, but imagined as perfect. You may possess a bit of compassion but, in your eyes, God is all-compassionate; likewise, you may have some measure of power, yet, from your limited vantage point, God is all-powerful.

Thus in this way you create an image of the Divine based on your idea of God in a perfect state. Actually, to glorify God, one projects upon one's representation of God qualities that are in oneself, though undeveloped, while at the same time trying to imagine how they could be in their Divine Perfection. In so doing, one is awakening, arousing, and perfecting them in one's personality! Perhaps without knowing it! Therefore prayer is the most creative of all acts. This is expressed in the saying "God created through your prayers as you"—in other words, your prayers are a way in which God is able to manifest as a reality, as you.

A concept from Jungian psychology helps to clarify further what I mean by awakening God's perfection within you. For instance, psychologists know that it is often the case that people project upon other people traits and characteristics that they have disowned within themselves. According to this theory, psychological maturity comes from "taking back" those projections by claiming responsibility for them within oneself. In the same way, spiritual maturity comes from accepting that despite the inevitable imperfections of earthly existence, it is still possible for us to seek to embody the richness of God's perfection.

So now, during this meditation practice, perhaps you could take the time to survey your life up to this point. Reflect upon the different periods in your life when certain qualities seemed to assume a great deal of importance to you—when everywhere you looked, you could see this quality exemplified in other people. Even the landscape seemed to mirror the quality you sought: the power, for example, that flashed through the lightning and thunder of a storm; the mood of peacefulness that radiated from the calm surface of a lake. As you watch your life unfold, you can also see how the qualities that you pursued changed throughout the course of your life. At certain periods, for instance, it might have been important to be of service, while at other stages of your life what mattered most was the attainment of mastery over a profession or pursuit. According to the Sufis, these various stages are called *maqams*.

Then, after surveying your life up to where you are now, try to attune to the quality that you intuit is trying to manifest through you at the present time. Just like the baby chicken trying to peck its way out through the shell, some attribute—whether compassion, wisdom, mercy, or power—is attempting to work its way through the limitations of your personality into the reality of life. Like a woman pregnant with her unborn child, if you don't nurture and support this tiny seed, it will be stillborn. And, just like the mother who knows she carries a child within her but who has not

yet seen its face, you may not be able to put your finger on the exact nature of this archetypal quality. There
is, however, an important midwife at work to assist in
the birth of this Divine Quality: the complex problems
and difficult issues of everyday life.

DISCOVERING
THE DIVINE QUALITIES HIDDEN
WITHIN YOUR PROBLEMS
∞

If you want to know what your qualities are, ask yourself what your defects and problems are. Behind the
everyday drama of life, deeper issues are being
enacted—and these issues always have to do with an
archetypal quality that is trying to manifest. Problems
are devices that can lead to what is behind your problem—the goal is to unmask them through meditation.
For if you judge your problems only at face value, then
you're not listening to what they are trying to communicate to you. Say, for example, that you are involved
in a conflict in which there is a lot of deception and
lying going on. One could imagine that seen through
the eyes of God, however, perhaps the reason fate has
placed you in the midst of this quandary is so that you
will be the one brave enough to speak aloud the truth
that has remained unspoken. Or, perhaps you are
caught in a situation in which there is a great deal of
suffering brought about by mean-spiritedness. Is the

antidote stern authority? Is it blurting out the truth unconcerned for the pain your words cause another? Or is it unconditional compassion? Sufism's way of dealing with life's problems is to attempt to see the quality underlying the situation in them that is struggling to be born. This is where the names of God help us throw more light on our problems.

For example, rather than ask, "What is the teaching of Sufism?" I prefer to ask, "What is it in the teaching that will help us to deal with these problems?" For this, there is nothing better than the practice of concentrating on qualities with which we are familiar, but imagining them in their perfect state as archetypes. This simply means repetition and reminiscence of what the Sufis call *sifat*, the Divine Qualities. According to the Qur'an, everything on earth has its correspondence in the Divine Treasury. These are archetypal images that lie behind reality as we know it: the idea of roundness, for example, from which the round table that we eat dinner on every night takes its expression; or the "rose ness" behind the real, red rose blooming in our garden.

It is important, however, to realize that these qualities are the devices through which God communicates His intention to us. According to Sufi teachings, such qualities are signs, *ayat*, that, like the tracks in the snow made by a bear that we have never seen, lead to the reality hidden behind the veil of what appears. There is a famous *ahadith*, for example, in which God says, "I was a secret treasure and loved to be known and therefore I created the Universe as a means of knowing myself."

Thus it was out of love that God descended from the solitude of unknowing into existence. As Rumi says, was it not out of love for the flower that the gardener cultivated the garden? One might add, was it not out of nostalgia for the beauty of forms that the architect drew up the blueprint of a monument?

Glorifying the Divine attributes of God as they manifest in existence is one of the central practices within the esoteric tradition of Sufism. According to this tradition, there are ninety-nine names, or attributes, of God in Arabic. They range across a spectrum of meaning from *ya Rahman*, Divine Magnanimity, to *Dhul Jelal wa Ikram*, the Lord of Majesty and Excellence. The advantage of reciting these phrases in a language which is foreign to most of us is that there is an opportunity for them to convey higher forms of meaning that lie out of range of our familiar language. Indeed, it is a great mistake to try to understand the exact translation of a particular name of God, as it reduces it to a linguistic construct. For myself, I much prefer translating them in terms of attributes that may gel into forms. That's extremely important in Sufism; it means embodying states of consciousness in the very flesh, blood, bones, and cells of our body—making God real.

Now, how does this apply to your meditation practice? Well, the idea is to develop a rapport between what you are doing in life and the corresponding qualities you are cultivating in your being. After attuning yourself through the preceding visualizations, mentally prepare yourself according to the previous steps above to deal with your problems. Then, review the specifics of those quandaries you are having a difficult time resolving. It might be, for example, that you feel other people are continually taking advantage of you. When you ask yourself if you are in control of your life, it seems clear that there are people who are stronger than you, or who are getting the best of you. Or, perhaps you have addictions, such as smoking cigarettes. You'd like to quit, but you can't because you fear terrible withdrawal symptoms. Yet if you had the courage to face those symptoms and stop smoking, you would develop a tremendous willpower. In both these situations, the quality that is lacking is mastery. Thus one way to strengthen this dimension of yourself is to repeat the two names of God in tandem: *ya Qabid*, constriction, and *ya Wali*, which means mastery. So one sees how one becomes limited by one's addiction and how strong one feels by mastering it.

Another example might be where one is experiencing guilt about the damage one might have caused another person by deceiving them. One may want to deny it because it's so demeaning to one's self-esteem. The antidote for this would be a combination of two names of God in tandem, *ya Munzil* and *ya Mu'izz*: discovering how bad one feels when one has acted dishonorably, and how good one feels when one has acted honorably. Restoring a sense of honor can pull oneself out of shame that has become paralyzing and has caused so much suffering. The image of honorability, even for the poor in spirit, was admirably illustrated in the poem of the donkey. Christ rode out on a donkey from the Garden of Gethsemane to the Temple of Solomon. The voice of honor speaking as the humble donkey said, "It's true, I have a raucous voice, and unseemly ears. But I did have my moment of glory when there were palms under my feet, and hallelujas all around me." That's the message of Christ: the poor in spirit participate in the glory of heavens.

Another quality one may work with is truth. Perhaps, for instance, you feel that what is holding you back in life is your fear that people will take advantage of your honesty, as children fear being punished in school for owning up. At the same time, something inside you is telling you that you've got to develop that quality or you will never become the person you long to be. But you feel stuck because you are afraid to tell people what you really think. So it helps to repeat the names of God in tandem: *ya Qahr* (Divine Sovereignty), *ya Haqq* (truth), or to be truthful by overcoming fear. Sometimes, it's a matter of feeling that you have a very limited amount of certain qualities. You might think that you possess a certain amount of willpower—but not much. Or a little bit of joy, intelligence, or truthfulness—but not much. Then, try to see how the situations in your life are directly related to those qualities you feel you lack—and are, in fact, trying to draw them forth from you as a way of moving you further along the path of spiritual evolution.

A Hindu story illustrates the way life repeatedly

forces us to change through seemingly impossible crises. In the old days in India when a husband died, the wife was supposed to throw herself onto the flames of the funeral pyre. Because there is a lot of illness in India, and women are kept in unsavory conditions, sometimes developing tuberculosis, it was often the case that an old man would marry a young woman. This was the situation of a young girl whose husband died. Naturally, she didn't want to throw herself on the funeral pyre; she was frightened of death. Someone sent her to a woman guru who had a pet cobra. This guru told her that if she could pet the cobra, she wouldn't have to go on the pyre. The trouble, however, said the guru, was that if the cobra senses fear it will bite you. A terrible predicament! Ultimately, although the young widow was frightened of the cobra, she knew that it was her one chance to live. So, in a tremendous test of her courage, she petted the cobra, which, because of her courage, did not bite her. The moral of this story is not only that the young widow was spared being sacrificed on the funeral pyre, but that through the crucible of this extreme circumstance she became a living testament to the power of human courage.

Though this story is set in a distant time and place, it recurs in different forms over and over again throughout the world: the woman whose husband has left her; a person who has cancer or AIDS; the child whose family is killed during war. I myself know what it is like to face danger. While in the Navy during World War II, I had the task of sweeping for mines at a time when our ships were being blown up by the Nazi U-boats. And, of course, there is the example of my sister, Noor, who, because of her daring work for the French underground, was captured by the Nazis and thrown into the Dachau concentration camp, where she was tortured and killed. I often think of how frightened she must have been—yet how courageous and committed she remained to the cause of freedom.

PARTICIPATING IN THE DRAMA OF THE UNIVERSE

Not all our difficulties are like those suffered in wartime, such as my sister's heroic, though tragic, fate. But just as epic struggles of war or famine are collective experiences that affect all of humankind, it is a mistake to think that our problems are ours alone. In fact, our private struggles are inextricably connected to our participation in the grand drama of the universe, and the setbacks and defeats we suffer are a reflection of the broader issues of our unique time and place in history.

Much like attuning to the mood of a powerful orchestral movement that stirs the depths of the heart, the collective, human dimension present in our everyday problems can stir the Divine Qualities to life within us. The pain of losing one's job, for instance, can lead to understanding how the jobless feel in a society

that values professionalism. The violation of one's freedom and individual rights can lead to a commitment
to truth and justice in the public arena. The emotions
do not always provide a direct route to the Divine
Qualities, however. Few of us, for example, have
escaped being marked by the wounds of resentment,
anger, and distress at life's terrible unfairness. In my
own case, as much as I would like to express God's mag-
nanimous and all-forgiving being, I must say that when
I think of the woman who gave away my sister, Noor,
to the Nazis for 100,000 francs, and the tragic conse-
quences it had, it's difficult for me not to feel resentment. Similarly, I've tried to forgive the Nazi who beat
and kicked her nearly to death, then left her to lie
bleeding throughout the night. What has made it
somewhat easier for me to understand how one human
being could do that to another is knowing that the
Nazis used psychopaths as jailers. Thus, when I consider the fact that the man might have been brought up
by a stepfather who was a drunk, or who beat him or
kicked him out of the house, my resentment is not as
easy to sustain. I have a more difficult time reconciling
with the woman who betrayed Noor's life for money.

How, then, can I teach forgiveness when it has
proved such a problem for me? My only answer lies in
the words of Christ, "They know not what they do."
His words make it easier for me to understand that such
people, like the Nazi and the Frenchwoman, do not
know what they're doing. I tell this deeply personal
story as part of my teachings on how important it is to

be able to forgive and let go. Probably we all have had experiences where we have been so badly maligned or abused by people that we find such an act very challenging. We have suffered abuse, and to be accused of not being able to forgive makes us feel even worse. It requires so much of us. Not being able to forgive, however, makes us more deeply entrenched in our suffering—we carry the wound in our hearts, and that stands in the way of our progress. Sometimes we have to open up these wounds and cleanse them.

Again, this is where the practice of *sifat*, or repetition of the Divine Qualities, is a kind of medicine. For instance, if one is riveted in one's despair, I would prescribe the names of God: *ya Daar* (O Thou who art testing me) in tandem with *ya Rahim* (compassion for those who are suffering even more). This expands your consciousness to include more and more of the Universe. Yet another practice that can help you overcome your personal sadness and open to the suffering of others is to place in tandem the names of God *ya Wasi* (embracing) and *ya Rahim* (compassion); while maintaining your personal center, as well as your personal feelings, extend your compassion in ever-widening circles. You feel that others who suffer are part of you; you embrace them. This practice makes it easier to deal with distress. Distress tends to make you feel constricted in your personal identity, but if you are thinking of the distress of the whole of humanity, or even just the sadness of people around you in your everyday life, you begin to realize how puny your concern for yourself is.

I myself think of the eleven-year-old girl in Bosnia who lost both arms and couldn't wash herself or eat. We have our suffering—but the suffering of other people is often unimaginably worse.

The Broken Heart: In fact, I often think the only way to deal with problems is to have a broken heart, to really feel broken about the suffering of people. I don't mean to put yourself in the place of a therapist who wants to help people, but rather to join in solidarity with the human condition and the depths of people's despair and suffering. For you can help a person only if you've gone through the same problems that he has gone through, and even if you have not solved them, you have found a way of living with them. Thus what you find in the end of searching for solutions to your problems is really love, because love breaks your heart—and that is the only power that can truly expand your consciousness. Love casts a different perspective on a problem and the way it looks. The names of God for this, again in tandem, are *ya Wadood* (love) and *ya Rahim* (compassion), the power of love that triggers compassion.

This kind of breakthrough in perspective cannot happen either through your will or your realization but through your emotional attunement. This means first allowing yourself to open up to the miracle of life, to be overcome by wonder at how extraordinary and amazing the phenomenon of existence is, with its good and its bad, its beauty and its horror, its terror and splendor. It means widening the vision of your heart so you see that a rotting banana peel is a banana peel, in the same way that you can discern the beauty in a person who appears cantankerous. The names of God for trying to see beauty where it may seem hidden are *ya Jemal* (beauty) and *ya Latif* (subtle). As you repeat these phrases, you cultivate within your heart the emotional sensitivity to the subtle beauty that transpires behind what appears to be ugly or repulsive.

Consider other levels of emotion, for example, the names of God *ya Malik*, kingliness or queenliness, and *ya Majid*, majesty. Repeated together, the repetition of these names of God focuses your heart on the reciprocal effect of these qualities upon each other to overcome sloppiness, permissiveness, and low self-respect. Imagine, for instance, the regal stature of a mountain range, a lion, elephant, king, or dervish; these are tangible, visible forms of these Divine Qualities. In the process of repeating *ya Malik, ya Majid*, you may experience emotions that range from feelings of wonder to the glorification of the Divine Majesty.

A further combination of qualities could be found in *ya Salaam* (peace) and *ya Baqi* (everlastingness). In this practice one shifts from identifying with that part of our identity which is constantly changing, to identifying with the essence within us which remains constant throughout time. Hazrat Inayat Khan, for instance, described a realization in an advanced meditation where one shifts one's identity from one's transient state of consciousness to one's deathless state—a shift that confers upon the meditator a sense of seren-ity and beatitude.

MAKING A PLEDGE
∞

Reflecting upon the mysterious, majestic grandeur of life as it manifests through the prism of your problems breaks down the barriers of your individual perspec-tive. Like a flower, you open toward life, committing to it despite all the suffering involved. Indeed, as life itself is the alchemical crucible within which the Divine Qualities mature to perfecting themselves, the inner work of meditation and reflection must be fol-lowed by an outer action that reinforces your commit-ment to a certain quality. Like a knight who kneels within a sacred sanctuary and who then places his left hand on his heart, his right hand forward, and pro-claims aloud his vow to serve the people of his ailing kingdom, so, too, can you make a solemn pledge to adjust the standard of your behavior so that it manifests the Divine Quality that is seeking to come into exis-tence through you.

The person who is frightened of speaking the truth, for example, might say, "All right—I know that my whole castle will break down if I say this. But I will say it anyway. Whatever happens, I'll say it—it's better if my house falls down than if it were built on something unsteady. Then I can build a better house on a solid foundation." That is the knightly way of cultivating within your personality the quality of truthfulness. Speaking your commitment out loud, then following it up by taking action in the outside world, helps intensify the quality of truth as it is trying to emerge from the void in the depth of your being.

There is no point, for example, in just repeating the name of God *ya Wali*, mastery, without implementing this quality in your personality. In fact, there's no point in repeating a name of God unless after saying it you can imagine a situation in your life in which this quality can be directly applied. Thus if you feel that you lack mastery over your life because you can't give up an addiction like cigarettes, then, after repeating *ya Wali*, you must make a pledge that you will no longer smoke—with the honest intention of quitting in order to gain control over your life. So a pledge is a commitment to apply certain qualities in certain situations. That means earmarking a certain situation in your life where you are not applying this quality as much as you could, and making a firm, verbal resolve that, from now on, "I will do this" or "I will not do this."

There is a metaphysical secret that lies behind the outer action of making a pledge. Hujwiri, a learned dervish who came to India more than a hundred years before the historic mission of the founder of our order, Khwaja Mu'inuddin Chishti, said, "The instant of time cuts the guilt of the past and the prefiguration of the future." That which cuts the continuity in time is a pledge. A pledge is done in an instant: "I have decided that I'm not going to do this anymore. I am going to do something different instead." That is a pledge. And from that moment on you have gained a certain amount of freedom because it cuts something of the conditioning of the past. And it might change your whole life! Because now, being a new person, your future is going to be different. The great instants in life are the times when we make a pledge. Suddenly there comes a situation, and you say, "I've had enough! I want to change." But a warning: You must be careful not to make a promise that you can't keep. For once you've made a pledge it will turn against you if you don't keep it.

REBIRTHING THE NEW SELF

∞

Every time you make a move to break old habits and move forward into the future, you are created anew. Like the mythical phoenix reborn from the flames, your new being has emerged out of the fiery pit of life's difficulties.

Instead of thinking, "This is me," a static and unchanging image, however, it is important to remember that the rebirthing process you have just been through is one that will continue to recur again and again. If you were aware of it, you would realize that you are continually in a state of being reborn and reformed. Just like the crocuses that break through the snow at the earliest onset of spring, so, too, are you always emerging anew. In order to contribute to the self-organizing faculty of the Universe, however, you have to be able to let go of your old self. The fresh petals in the center of the flower cannot unfold until the decaying petals fall away. The Sufi teaches to resurrect before dying. Thus if you hang on to your personality, you will never change: you will go backward instead of evolving forward. Though this is often emotionally painful, the understanding that what is emerging is not only you but the richness of the whole Cosmos will out-weigh your suffering.

Still, now that you have reached a point in your meditation when you feel that something has really clicked—the feeling that this is the "real me" and this is the quality that I embody—it may seem perplexing to be told that you are continually changing. Confused, you might then wonder, "How do I know this is really me?" One way of understanding this process is to compare yourself to a musical theme on which a com-poser makes endless variations. Or, you could think of your personal self as a medium through which the Universe is particularized—God become human. The theologian Pierre Teilhard de Chardin called this "hominization"; in other words, it is all One Being, but that Being is particularized by fragmenting Himself into a multitude of beings who are like endless varia-tions on a theme. In the Jewish Bible translated by Churaki, the voice of Yahweh speaking from the

Burning Bush doesn't say, "I am who I am," but "I am that I become."

PERENNITY

∞

The Instant of Time: In fact, we are a "continuity in change," or "perennity." As I said, it's never the same water that flows under the bridge, yet it's the same river; so, too, is our real being evolving yet eternal. In metaphysical terms, the Sufis explain this as the difference between everlastingness and eternity: everlastingness is in the realm of the existential and temporal, while the eternal is the realm of intelligence beyond consciousness.

The yogic practice called *pranayama* is a breathing practice that will help you to directly experience these two modes of consciousness: the way you are in your eternal, impersonal, and unchanging dimension as well as that part of you that is constantly revolving and evolving through life situations that act as a catalyst for the Divine Qualities to become activated as your personality. To begin, place the thumb of your right hand under your chin, and the middle finger of your right hand next to the right nostril, but don't immediately press it. Then place the palm of your left hand against the back of your right hand, and the thumb of your left hand against your left nostril again, without pressing upon it. You can start by just . . . exhaling . . . then . . .

inhaling, each time a little longer than the last. Then, after inhaling, press both fingers and hold your breath; following this pause, exhale through both nostrils. Now, press the middle finger of the right hand while releasing the thumb of your left hand, and inhale through the left nostril. Hold your breath; press both fingers. Then exhale through the right nostril. Now inhale through the right nostril. Hold your breath; exhale through the left nostril, then inhale through both nostrils. As you hold your breath this time, turn your eyeballs upward, curl your tongue, and press the bottom of your tongue against your palate.

What we are doing with the breath is creating a pendulum of energy that is swinging from the left to the right, and then from the right to the left. The moment when the swing is in a state of suspense, like when a pendulum hangs suspended, is that instant when the breath is held and time stands still. After repeating this breathing practice several times, you can begin to add the following concentrations. Because these meditations may be difficult to incorporate in just one breath, you may want to meditate on them first, then try harmonizing them with the breath.

So, to begin, when you inhale through your left nostril, recollect your past. Think of all the events in your life and how they have unfolded in their chronological sequence. At the same time, think of how you have changed and evolved over the course of time through certain major life events. For example, after the failure of a relationship, perhaps, you experienced pain. Or, after having been let down by someone important to you, cautiousness set in. Then, in a change of tack, try to see the impact of your personality on events. One way of doing this is by remembering what you were like when a certain event occurred, then compare it to how you are now. This naturally leads you to the realization that if the same situation happened all over again today, it would not happen the same way because you have changed. If you do this practice every day, you will gain insight into yourself. In Buddhism, this is called "observing the self."

Reviewing the past is followed naturally by the motion forward into the future. What is the future? It is an ever-receding horizon made up of dreams of what you would like to be and what you would like to have happen, yet with trepidation and misgivings as to how feasible they are and the obstacles you will have to surmount. Yet what else but hope for the future can pull us out of the limitations of the past? Hopes and wishes are not enough, however—they must be embodied in the pledge to do things differently from this moment forward, whether it is stopping a certain behavior or continuing to do something that you have always done, but with more zest.

The time to make this pledge is at that peak instant when you hold your breath after completing the inhalation. There are no frontiers to this instant, no boundaries toward the past or the future; it peters off at both sides. This is because time is not linear. It is like space, which is landscaped by gravitation; it can grind to a stop and start up again, just like an apostrophe in music where everything pauses before the next movement begins. These dynamics help explain why a vow made during an instant of time has the power to break the continuity of the past so that something new can emerge to change the direction of your life path. This confirms Hujwiri's adage "The instant of time is a sharp sword that cuts the guilt of the past and the prefiguration of the future."

Putting this in the language of psychology, guilt always refers to a past that continues into the present. There are certain conditions in life, for example, when you find yourself in a state of suspense, in a crisis where you know you simply can't go on the same way that you have so far. You don't know yet exactly how you are going to change but you know that you have reached a stage where there must be a dramatic turnaround. I am not talking about a change in circumstances but a change in your way of thinking. It is during this instant of time—that state of suspense when the breath is held and you are free from the influences of both the past and the future—that you can make a pledge to commit yourself to turning over a new leaf. Like catching a fresh breeze at sea, this gives you the impetus to make a new start; with the suddenness of a boat changing tack, you can feel your life change direction. Because from the moment that you have made this pledge, you are a different person. You have strengthened yourself and now proceed by leaps and bounds. This will have a corresponding effect on your surrounding circumstances because the effects of the past have been interrupted by your pledge: the past has finally lost its power over you.

Then, as you exhale through the right nostril, project yourself forward into the new horizon that has now opened up as a result of your pledge. You feel freed up, as if something within you that has been held in abeyance has been unfettered; suddenly, there is a flowering in your being. You can see situations in your life that have been stuck begin to flow forward, and your spirit dances with joy. That is the way to find joy in your suffering. Suffering is always connected with the past, and joy is connected with the future. Now, do the same concentration, only in reverse direction. Breathing in through the right nostril, you can see that just the way the past triggers off some conditioning on the present and, by the same token, the future, so, too, do your preconceived expectations for the future impose limitations on your freedom. Thus after your inhalation in through the right nostril, hold the breath, using that instant of suspended time to free yourself from your dependence upon your projections for the future. Then, breathing out through the left nostril, realize that the past is no more what it was and has changed by your changing. And what is more, your changing affects your future. This practice could be called calibrating the past and the future, seeing the connection between the two with great insight.

Now you breathe in through both nostrils, hold your breath, then exhale through both nostrils. Instead of oscillating from the past to the future, and using the retroactive influence of the future upon the past, you are shifting from transiency to eternity. Thus you represent yourself as the whole pendulum—that is, you are the weighted pole that is moving in time and space, but also the point where the pendulum is suspended, unchanged. Then, as you inhale, think that what you have gained in knowledge through your achievements in life is never lost. Instead, it is transmuted into the essence of wisdom; this becomes incorporated into the Divine programming, contributing to the evolution of the world. To do this practice, think of yourself as a flower that, after discarding its dross of old petals and leaves, is transmuted into perfume.

So at the end of inhaling through both nostrils, you are discovering the everlastingness (in Sufi terms, *Baqa*) of your being that survives its transiency. When you hold your breath, you have a sense of having hoisted your consciousness beyond existence to the backstage of the world, so to speak. This is what is meant by eternity (in Sufi terms, *Samad*). You are touching upon the peak of your being, which remains unchanged, even while everything else continuously changes. There you discover the originating motivation behind the Cosmos that remains unchanged—this is where one's fate originates. We sometimes call it destiny, which contrasts with our free determination, just as the unchanging contrasts with the changing.

Now, when we exhale through both nostrils, we see how our free will develops as the branches unfold from a tree. This image reflects the way our free will has a certain scope of expression, while at the same time it is inextricably connected to the interests of the whole.

Awakening your new being will free you from your dependence upon those strategies of the psyche that have so far held you back, enabling you to deal with the challenges of life from your deeper self. Your pride in the discovery that your will participates in customizing the programming of the Universe is what will endow you with the energy you need to pursue those ideals, or qualities, that you serve. Do not allow the views of others to stand in the way of your free will to become what you are becoming. That is counterproductive. However, it is helpful to keep an ear open in case the opinion of another person opens a perspective on the problem that you had not seen before. Honor the way you are evolving, for this is the way you are fulfilling your sacred covenant to serve the Divine Sovereignty on earth.* Never think that this is a task that can be fully completed, however; instead, like a spiritual

---

* A *sura* of the Qur'an called *sura al-ikhlas* says *lam yalid*, "He does not beget." The Muslim profession of faith says *la ilaha illa 'llah*, "no Divinity except God." However, the Qur'an says, "We [that is, God, the plural voice] are the inheritor of the earth and of those who are there" (15:23).

If He is the archetype of which I am an exemplar, and in this case the Inheritor of the bounty of the Universe, I am the exemplar of that inheritance (like His Kingship, *malikiya*, is the model for my kingliness). Therefore I need to actuate that inheritance in my personality features, however unequally to that perfect model—not the way that the son inherits the idiosyncrasies of his father or mother, but in a different relationship, which is that of an archetype to an exemplar.

mountaineer, you will always be pulled onward by a nostalgia for the Mount Olympus of the future.

As my father, Hazrat Inayat Khan, put it, the natural instinct to grow and move forward is driven by a "passion for the unattainable." That is, the future is like the horizon that is always just a little bit farther, drawing you on to reach beyond yourself. This quest is what makes beings great; by definition, these are the extraordinary individuals who refuse to accept that a dream or an ideal is in any way impossible to achieve. In fact, the word impossible is not even in the Divine dictionary! That is why the greatest challenge facing humankind is to take that which seems impossible— and make it actual.

BUILDING A TEMPLE FOR THE DIVINE PRESENCE:

TRADITIONAL SUFI PRACTICES

"We are building the palace for the king, wherein the king must live."

— HAZRAT INAYAT KHAN

"This is not my body, it is the temple of God; this is not my heart, it is the altar of God."

— HAZRAT INAYAT KHAN

◆

The Sufis of the Chishti Order are linked by initiation through a chain of teachers, known as the *Silsila*. My teacher was my father, Hazrat Inayat Khan; his teacher was Hazrat Sayyid Abu Hashim Madani, a successor in the lineage of the Chishti *Silsila* in India. The esoteric principle behind the *Silsila* is that of

transmission. In other words, at the moment of initiation, a kind of spiritual energy passes through the
teacher to the student, investing him with a sacred
charge.

Just before Hazrat Sayyid Abu Hashim Madani
died, for instance, he directed Pir-O-Murshid Inayat
Khan, his successor, to go to the West and attune
the hearts of people to the music of the soul. At that
time, my father was a renowned Indian musician; he
gave up a career in music for the sake of the work he
had been given to found the Sufi Order in the West.
But the essence of music is rhythm, harmony, and
attunement, and, like a subtle perfume, these qualities
pervade all of his teachings. He even said, "Be not sur-
prised if the message of the future is given in the form
of music." This universal orientation is the motivation
behind the broad outlook of the Sufi Order founded by
Pir-O-Murshid Hazrat Inayat Khan in the West, pio-
neering a whole new way of introducing spirituality
into everyday life. That is, using the language of the
"music of the soul" to communicate a universal message that erupts from that chrysalis which is the Sufi
Order.

"Introducing spirituality into everyday life" is a
phrase that is used a lot these days. What it means to
me is something profoundly real: building a temple to
invite the Divine Presence as a living reality on earth.
People with a very refined nature, for instance, often
experience a deep need for the sacred. This need most

often has been met by religious institutions that create a psychological environment by means of physical devices favorable to a holy attunement. Yet in a world where mundane pursuits have taken over more and more of our time, this rarist and most precious of attunements is an increasingly fleeting experience. In the same way, the complexities of modern life have made it difficult for many to retire in seclusion to a spiritually ideal environment like Mount Athos or a cave in the Himalayas.

Since historically, however, Sufis, just like the early Jews, often have lived a nomadic lifestyle, with no temple or mosque to rely upon, they became quite skilled at learning how to fashion temples out of their physical and subtle bodies. Just as musicians rely upon their instruments to make music, Sufis came to rely upon certain esoteric practices as a way of attuning to the sacred. In the same way, it is possible for the modern seeker to enter the world within through the doorway of the creative imagination, as well as through mystical techniques of attunement. By symbolically donning the garb of a pilgrim, attuning to the consciousness of a hermit, and visualizing ourselves secluded deep in a cave or faraway temple, we activate the contemplative archetype—that part of us that seeks the holiest of the holy.

One of the latest findings in physics helps to explain the spiritual mystery that I am trying to convey. An electron can exist only if circumstances are created that favor its appearance; before that, it exists only in a "virtual" state. This is the same principle behind Hazrat Inayat Khan's phrase "Make God a reality." If we don't create a place for the Divine in the here and now of our daily lives, the Divine will continue to exist in a state of virtuality, or potentiality.

Thus the central challenge in Sufism is that of awakening God—not just in us but as us. Therefore, our body participates in our experience. Since our bodies carry within their very structure and cellular memory the circular motion of the stars, planets, and galaxies, these latent forces are aroused when the body rotates—as in the whirling of the dervishes, or the movement of one's head and chest rotating around one's heart center in the practice of the *dhikr*, a ritual of remembrance for inviting the Divine Presence into the chamber of the heart. Based on the repetition of the Arabic phrase *La ilaha illa 'llah hu*—"There is no Divinity except God"—this practice includes circular movements of the head and body.

Like the bricks and mortar that build a physical church, *dhikr* and whirling are the tools by which meditators can construct for themselves out of the fabric of their bodies a body of light, a vessel for the Divine Presence on earth. This practice, therefore, leads to making one God-conscious.

ENTERING THE CONSCIOUSNESS
OF A DERVISH
∞

Before beginning these practices, it helps to attune to the consciousness of a dervish. The archetype of the dervish is rather difficult to describe: they are very mysterious beings who are high from their concentration on the Divine Being. It is a very different attunement from that of the *rishi* high up in the Himalayas. The dervish can be sitting in the marketplace on a heap of banana peels, and still be in a state of ecstasy. He doesn't have to flee the world in order to experience spirituality right here and now.

The dervish Sufi Shams of Tabriz expressed this poignant union of Divine Perfection and human limitation when he said, "The man of God (the dervish) is a palace in a ruin." The image of a palace in a ruin conveys the kind of majesty or grandeur embodied by a dervish, who represents the challenge of the higher self as it is lacerated and damaged by the selfishness of the world, yet somehow is still able to manifest Divine Glory and Power.

I can tell you my own personal story of an encounter with a dervish. I was traveling in India in search of awakening when, having settled in for the night, I ordered tea and was told that someone would return right away with it—only to sit waiting as the hours passed. Finally, night arrived, and, giving up hope of a hot cup of tea, I put my sleeping bag on the floor and

went to sleep. Then, in the middle of the night, a raucous voice screeched, and there was a loud pounding on
the door. "Good God," I thought—and went straight
back to sleep. When my cup of tea finally arrived the
next morning, I asked who had been shaking my door
down, only to be told that a dervish had come to
awaken me. The next night, when the same thing happened, I ran to the door but the dervish had already fled
into the darkness. Just imagine, I came all the way to
India to be awakened, and this time missed my chance.

The next day I traveled to the Dargah, or memorial
shrine, of the founder of the Chishti Order, Hazrat
Moinuddin Chishti, in the city of Ajmer. The enchant-
ment of that tomb is incredible: it is a beautiful building with a marble floor. People are all around, playing
music, sleeping, or praying. The whole atmosphere is
otherworldly. I was sitting there bemoaning the fact
that I had missed my encounter with the dervish.
Suddenly, behind me, I heard a voice say, "You there,"
in such a terrifying manner that I didn't have the
courage to turn my head. Yet all of a sudden, I was
awakened! That's a dervish—he is trying to reveal the
secret of what is called the secret treasure, a mystery of
God that both desires to be known and yet is covered
over by all the things that constantly preoccupy us and
distract us from the real thing. Like a Zen priest who
provokes bewilderment and confusion in his student by
assigning him a riddle-like *koan*, or who raps him on
the shoulder with a cane, a dervish's rude and uncon-

ventional behavior is intended to shock us out of our mindless complacency—awakening us to the true nature of reality. And that is the purpose of these practices—to wake us up to the magnificent revelation of the Divine Presence as it is manifesting in this very moment.

WHIRLING*

∞

To begin the practice of whirling, you might call to mind images of the Turkish Order of the Mevlevi Whirling Dervishes. Dressed in white robes, crowned with their tall, cone-shaped felt hats, arms outstretched, they appear as graceful as a host of luminous stars and planets spiraling through the galaxies of the Cosmos. But despite the fact that images of whirling dervishes have become sprinkled throughout popular culture, it is important to remember that whirling is not a dance, or a performance. Instead, it is a sacred, ritual movement grounded in the religious context of Islam, and it originated more than 700 years ago in Turkey with the Sufi poet Jelaluddin Rumi.

---

* Safety warning: To prevent any physical injuries, it may be useful, when first starting this practice, to have a "safety guard" who can catch you should you get too dizzy and fall down. In addition, people who have high blood pressure, a heart condition, or any other physical impediment should refrain from doing this practice.

According to history, Rumi was renowned for his scholarly knowledge; in our time, he would be similar to a popular university professor with many students. One day, however, an ecstatic dervish named Shams of Tabriz visited him. He took the scholarly manuscript Rumi had been working on and threw it in a well, saying that if Rumi was offended, he could take it out again and it would be dry. But Rumi declined; from that moment Rumi became one of the greatest poets and mystics of Sufism. It is said that later, his jealous disciples killed Shams. Distraught with grief, Rumi absented himself from his *khanqah*, isolating himself from his community. He sought his friend among the glittering stars in the vast sky, lost in a vision of the choreography of the heavens. Rumi then returned to his disciples and introduced them to the practice of whirling, in which he figured as the sun and each of his disciples a particular planet. It was even said that he had a particular melody or rhythm for each planet, but that knowledge has been lost over time.

The practice of whirling as it has come down to us from Rumi begins with the traditional, beautiful dervish greeting in which the arms are crossed like St. Andrew's cross. Attuning to the majestic qualities of the dervish, place your right toe on top of your left toe, cross both arms over your heart, place the hand of each arm on the opposite shoulder, and bow reverently. Then, as you raise yourself, uncross your feet. Next, start whirling counterclockwise (to the left). Place the weight of your body on your left foot. Next, lift your right foot and turn it toward your left foot—so that you are pigeon-toed. Now, rotate your left foot, using your right foot to occasionally touch the ground, propelling you and helping you to maintain your balance. The axis around which you are spinning is between the big toe of your left foot and the next toe. In Konya, they actually place a nail in the floor between these two toes—it helps them to locate the point around which they gravitate as they spin.

As you slowly begin to spin, keep the motion very steady, rotating to the left in a counterclockwise direction. After establishing your balance, gradually unfold your arms, outstretching them like an eagle spreads its wings. Keep your right hand turned upward, and your left hand downward. Of course, you are going to feel dizzy. With everything moving rapidly around you, reality seems upended and nothing is where you think it is. But this is not a bad thing; instead, it is a good lesson in *maya*, or the illusory nature of the created world. As a consequence, you find that you can't rely on the outside to get your bearings; however, if there is a horizontal line in the hall—if, for example, the windows are at the same height—that will give you a sense of where the horizon is. To keep your balance as you whirl, concentrate on the knuckle of the index finger of your left hand—don't look outward at the surrounding environment, just keep your attention on this knuckle. Sometimes whirling a little faster makes you feel less dizzy; it's only when you slow down that you may feel as if the earth is coming to hit you in the face.

As you progress in this practice over time, the result is that you begin to feel that you are like a planet or star whirling in synchrony with the infinitely spiraling motion of the Cosmos. As you let yourself go into outer space, while at the same time staying grounded through your feet planted on the earth, you feel transported into a state of ecstasy and freedom. To link your experience of the Cosmos to your life situation, you might like to choose a planet that you feel represents certain qualities in your nature, or that you would like to strengthen, such as Mercury if you feel quick-moving and inspired; Saturn for qualities of wisdom or practicality; or Jupiter for majesty or sovereignty. The practice of whirling closes by slowly coming to a stop, then repeating the dervish bow. Standing in motionless silence, you may continue to feel the spinning of the Universe around you. If you feel dizzy, just place a finger close to your eyes; this gesture has a steadying effect and keeps you close to the center of your being.

THE *DHIKR*

∞

Now let us share in the practice of the *dhikr*, which does not entail whirling your whole body but simply rotating your head and chest around your heart center. Like whirling, the beauty of this practice is that the whole body participates in the mystical experience of the

Divine. Through the combination of the repetitive motion of the body with the recitation of the *dhikr*— either silently, on the breath, or aloud—we are using our bodies as temples. On an even subtler energy level, we are building temples of light out of the fabric of our aura and a temple of magnetism out of electromagnetic fields, with our heart as the altar in this temple. Compared to the practice of *samadhi*, where the devotee must sit motionless in an *asana*, or meditative posture, the *dhikr* is about awakening in life, in the body, rather than beyond life.

The basic practice is as follows: Sit cross-legged in the traditional meditative pose. On the exhalation of the breath, turn the head in a half circle from the left shoulder, circling downward to the left knee, then moving to the right knee, then upward to the right shoulder. Continue to rotate the head to the zenith. As you are making this circular motion, think of the words *La ilaha*, or, in English, "There is no other Divinity." Then, on the inhalation, turn your head downwards toward the solar plexus, immediately raise your head straight up again in line with the spine, passing in review its different *chakras*, and finally culminate at the crown center with the face turned upward. With this second motion, think the second half of the phrase, *illa 'llah*—"except God." Now hold your breath and turn your head toward your physical heart, thinking the word *hu*. In Arabic, *hu* means him, as well as a person who is absent. The Sufi al Hallaj, for instance, says that when several people are in a room concentrating on a person who is not there, that person is more present than the people concentrating.

The reason for concentrating on the physical heart in the left of the chest, rather than the cardio plexus in the center of the chest, is because the *dhikr* is a further extension of the breathing practices where the thrust of the breath continues to flow in the human circulatory system. This could be illustrated by the way the power of a locomotive is communicated to the wheel in a position which is offset from the center of the wheel. This is the way in which awakening in life is instilled into body functions in a psychic motion, just like the physical, circular motion of the stars.

The phrase *La ilaha illa 'llah hu*, or, in English, "There is no Divinity except God," is Arabic, and derives from the pre-Islamic language which is also the origin of the Hebrew language. After you have accustomed yourself to the repetition of the *dhikr* along with the physical motions of the upper body, you may add the following concentrations. These concentrations build upon and incorporate the meditations in the previous chapters, transforming the repetition of the *dhikr* into a direct experience of various altered states of consciousness.

Circumnambulating the Temple: Expand the nonphysical dimensions of your body, thereby strengthening the subtler configuration of your electromagnetic field—extend this to your aura. So, as you whirl your head downward to the left, around, and back up, imagine that you are creating a centrifuge of energy that is pushing the grosser elements of your being to the outside of the circle you are circumscribing; this is the centrifugal force. After you bring your head down, raise it up again. One could compare the condition, when your head is turned toward the zenith, with that of a pail of water that one rotates. If it is rotated fast enough, the water will not spill when it is upside down. This represents the most precarious position. At that point you feel the pull of the center of your being. This is where the centripetal forces take over the centrifugal. Consequently, your head is turned toward the solar plexus.

These centrifugal and centripetal forces represent respectively the cosmic dimension of your being, and on the other hand the interior space within the center of your being. As you continue to repeat this practice, differentiate between these alternating forms of energy: a sense of scattering and dispersal of energy on the *la ilaha*, then, on the *illa*, a pull toward the center, and on the phrase *'llah hu*, experiencing one's consciousness being raised toward the zenith. The zenith, or the point above the head, is a state of precarious equilibrium: We have already experienced it in the "ha" at the end of *ilaha*, and now we experience it once more in the "h" of *'llah*. Thus, there is a suspense with the "h" of the *'llah* when the head is turned toward the zenith. But this is followed by a descent of the head, turning this time to the physical heart while intoning the syllable *hu*, which

Pir Vilayat Inayat Khan

means "Him (God) present in my heart." Now continue to repeat the entire cycle in a continuous flow of motion.

This particular concentration of the *dhikr* enacts the practice of initiates who were required to circumnambulate the temple before entering. On the first half-circle of the *dhikr*, imagine that you are building a temple around your heart, preparing yourself to enter. As you are circling your heart you are building a temple out of the electromagnetic field. Then, on the downward motion, turn your consciousness inward, as if, after this initial preparation, you have finally entered the inner sanctum of your temple. Like stepping off a crowded street into the hushed atmosphere of a church, crossing the threshold of this temple marks a definite transition from the profane to the sacred. The electromagnetic field encircling you serves as a layer of protection against the distractions of the outside world, enabling you to dive deeper within yourself. A good model for the depth of concentration you feel at this point is the image of Buddha sitting in the middle of a storm; you have a sense of being able to touch upon an inner peace that suffuses your being from within.

Entering the Temple of Light: Now you are going to build a temple of light through the practice of the *dhikr* of light. As you continue to focus on the image of your body as a temple, visualize your aura as an aureole of luminous light. As you trace the motion of your head downward and around, imagine that the radiance of

178

your aura extends far beyond your physical location, reaching right out into the star-studded cosmic ocean of light. When you turn inward toward your solar plexus, you realize that the cells of your body are constantly absorbing light from the surrounding environment, including cosmic rays from outer space. Thus the cells of your body both absorb and transmit light which is radiated as your aura into the environment. Indeed, in its purely physical aspect, your aura is made up of the radiation of this sparkling light. The brain is lit up from within. This light is conducted through the optic nerves, which are an extension of the brain. The middle-range frequencies of light in the brain cannot pass through the skull, and therefore it is only the high-frequency ultraviolet light which passes through the skull at a point in the brain that is sometimes mistaken for the third eye. The real third eye is in the pineal gland. Though you can't see this with your physical eyes, you can use your imagination to visualize your body and aura as an actual structure of light that, like a hologram, exists in space.

The regular, architectonic motion of the *dhikr* enhances the luminosity and structure of this radiant composition. As your head goes round in the circle, imagine that you are tensing a bow in preparation to shoot an arrow. Then, at the dramatic moment when the head goes down, release the bow, shooting an arrow of light from your third eye into the solar plexus. This causes a sparkling to erupt, an outburst of scintillating light from within that reaches right up along the spine, lighting up each of the *chakras* and culminating at the top of the head in an explosion of fireworks. This splendid illumination then coalesces in the wonderful radiance of your heart that has become illumined like the sun. Indeed, you could say that at this moment, the Cosmos has given birth to the sun in your heart. This spiritual experience is the inner meaning of the phrase "a light upon a light," which figures in a *sura* of the Qur'an (24:35).

At this stage, you can now do the *dhikr* of light (though still remaining seated), intensifying the spinning, circular motion that has been put into effect with this practice. As you exhale on the *la ilaha*, for example, rotate your upper body clockwise around the pivot that is centered in the solar plexus. First, describe a violet circle with your third eye, accompanied by a blue radiance of your eyes. Then, to add to that, imagine that your crown center is circumscribing a circle with diamondlike colorless light irradiated with flashing hues; within that, draw a golden circle with your heart *chakra*. Through the sheer force of repetition of these circles of light, numberless bands of hues aligned in concentric circles like the spectrum of a rainbow will gradually widen into ever-extending spirals and vast vortices of light.

Now, move your head and upper body forward and downward on the inhalation of the breath, then upward again, eventually returning to the left and right motion as you exhale. Now, as you inhale, your head turns toward the solar plexus and moves upward as previously described. The experience of spinning through the galaxies is so moving, the encounter with the glory of the Cosmos so awe-inspiring, that you are filled with the ecstatic spirit of a dervish. Even from your vantage point on earth, you are dancing, revolving like a star in the choreography of the light of the heavens!

Indeed, beyond experiencing the bliss of the physical splendor of light lies the emotion of light—a feeling of being deeply stirred by the magic of illumination. As you concentrate on the heart *chakra* while you hold your breath on the pause between the inhalation and the exhalation, you feel your heart quickened by the breath of pure spirit. After concentrating on your physical heart, turn your attention to your heart *chakra* and represent it as the altar in the temple. As the light from the heavens descends, it meets the light emerging from the inside, and the two congregate on the altar in your heart in the center of this temple. This ignites an exaltation of the spirit, suffusing you in an ecstasy of light. You have an impression that something absolutely magnificent is about to transpire: a cosmic celebration in which you are the temple, its radiance, the altar, and also the priest, officiating in a cosmic celebration.

If you can hold your breath long enough, you could now pause with your glance in its normal horizontal direction. You will now experience your aura as a whirling temple of light that both radiates light and protects you. This radiating force comes from within your heart; an eternal flame that burns brightly from within, the center, where one awakens in life rather than beyond life.

Spectrums of Consciousness: Though the *dhikr* is a succinct phrase conveying the essential, powerful spiritual truth that all is God, each of its syllables encompasses various spectrums of consciousness. Like doorways, these sounds usher the initiate on a journey through the different planes—then back to life, transformed and renewed by a new vision of reality.

As already stated, the first phrase, *la*, in which you move a half-circle from the left shoulder to the knees and up to the right shoulder, for instance, fashions the arc of a circle that gives you the sense of the choreography of the galaxies in a continual, circular motion. Then, on the *ilaha*, moving from the right shoulder to the top of the head, in addition to encompassing the vastness of the Cosmos, you are encompassing the vastness at all the planes, or levels, of your being.

Then, as you bring your head down, the sound *illa* resonates in your solar plexus. When this sound is uttered in the traditional manner of the dervishes—a short, sharp, penetrating vowel sound that comes from the back of the throat—it can produce a very strident sound like striking glass. In India, for example, it is not unusual for people to be awakened from their sleep by dervishes miles away repeating this phrase of the *dhikr*. The reason for this is because the solar plexus is where we are the most emotionally vulnerable; it is the seat of pain and tension. Thus bringing this sound down into the solar plexus is like performing surgery on our deepest wounds. In Islam, for instance, it is said that Muhammad had something removed from his heart, then found himself completely transformed. In Sufism, this process is called the purification of the heart. So, as you repeat the word *illa*, imagine that you are being released from everything that stands in the way of your union with God. As the Sufi mystic al Hallaj uttered at this moment, "O take away this 'I am' between Thou and me that so irks me."

In Sufi mysticism this is called *fana*, which means annihilation, as there can be no rebirth without a dark night of the soul, a total annihilation of all that you believed in and thought that you were. It is similar to the stage in the alchemical process called *solve et coagule*, dissolve and coagulate. On the most day-to-day level, it corresponds to a time of complete breakdown when everything goes wrong: your relationship ends; you have an accident; your health breaks down; you lose your job. Locating these seemingly horrendous events within the context of a spiritual transformation helps you to know that you are not just a helpless victim at the mercy of random forces, but that the Universe is guiding you through a mystical process of rebirthing. By trusting in this transformative process, aligning yourself with it rather than forcefully resisting it, breakdown can become breakthrough. Or, as Hazrat Inayat Khan says, "A defeat can aver itself to be a victory." It helps to keep this in mind whenever you are going through a crisis—because in the end, you will see that what you had thought was a complete reversal of fortune turned out to be the dawn of a new self more aligned with the purpose for which you were born.

So, to return to the *dhikr*, when you thrust your head sharply toward the solar plexus, you are experiencing a collapse, a total breakdown of the self. Then, as the head rises slowly on the drawn-out phrase *'llah*, you begin an ascent through the different planes of consciousness. As your head is raised from being turned toward the solar plexus, you will be attuning to one plane after another. At the beginning of this journey, you feel a break-through that is the first glimpse of the emergence of your new personality out of the ashes of your old self. This creative moment is captured in the name of God *Muhyi*, which means to regenerate. Every time one is reborn, something new needs to come through. In Sufism, this level, or stage of consciousness, is called *Mithal*. It corresponds to the realm of metaphor and image in which thoughts become translated into forms. The instrument that facilitates this process of translating ideas and inspiration into form is the creative imagination. The name of God applied here is *ya Khaliq* (the Creator). There are further practices: *ya Bari* (the Evolver) and *ya Musawwir* (the Fashioner).

This is not fantasy: what you are doing is individualizing the Divine Imagination as it manifests through you in a unique way. You have the sense that "the whole Cosmos is coming through me in a particular way." That is exactly what is happening. It's at this level of consciousness of difference, diversity, and imagination that we discover the nature of our special contribution to the totality rather than being wholly immersed in it. It's that creative moment when you feel especially keenly that "the pull of the future is stronger than the push of the past." At this stage, you are facing forward, rather than being pulled back by regret or sorrow over the past. It's a moment when, seized by possibility and potentiality, you ask yourself, "What if?" or, "What if I were different?" or, "What if I should be what I would be if I could be what I might be?"

As you ascend further, you raise your consciousness into the next level that, according to the Sufis, is called *Malakut*, or the celestial spheres. Incidentally, we think of these planes as elsewhere, whereas they are perspectives monitored by the way we focus our consciousness. This could be illustrated by a hologram in which there are superimposed images—but we can see only one image at a time. To do this we need to simply shift our focus. But these images are present within the hologram just like the planes are present in our world. This plane of consciousness, *Malakut,* is where we experience the dimension of ourselves that exists, as it always has, in its original perfection. To capture a sense of the consciousness of this stage, you may need to enter into the attunement of the child inside you. Or, you may reflect on the hierarchies of beings of light and archangels. On earth, the celestial spheres break through in those rare moments when something heavenly seems about to transpire, such as the light in the eyes of a baby cradled by a mother, or a beautiful action in an ugly situation.

Thus it is a state of meditation where you actually recover the memory of your state prior to your birth. Buddha pointed out that the memory of the Cosmos is still present in our unconscious but has been interrupted at the moment of birth.

Recovering that memory of the heavenly realms is a pivotal moment: suddenly you remember who you really are—a celestial being who descended into earthly conditions, then lost the memory of your true identity. As I have said, this was enacted by the initiates of Eleusis who, during the course of their initiation, suddenly awakened to their original nature as a Divine Being of light. Indeed, this stage of consciousness is like stepping out of a world of shadows and illusion into a familiar but long-forgotten world of light. I'm not talking about only physical light here, but a recollection that triggers off a state of consciousness in which we realize that we are much more than what we thought we were in our human limitations. It is that breathtaking "aha!" moment when you encounter the beauty and illumination of your celestial counterpart.

At the same time, your experiences as a human being on planet earth have changed who you were as you existed in pre-eternity: in other words, your soul has been enriched through your human experience, while at the same time it has become tarnished due to the desires of the ego and the harsh influences of the world. As we explored in the previous chapter about problems, you are not static and unchanging, but a continuing work-in-progress. Now, I am talking about a dimension of yourself that is between eternal and transient, which Hazrat Inayat Khan calls everlasting. One way of grasping this is to review all the events in your life since you were a child, seeing yourself as a continuity in change, as we have already encountered previously. Now look at them from an overview and see how you remember the gist of the experience rather than the details. So, like the perfume of flowers, the essence survives the passage of time. Everlastingness is remembering the quintessence of an experience. In other words, in this experience, your life experiences become transmuted, like the distillation in alchemy. It is the meaning of resurrection. This is exactly what occurs when, in meditation, you sift through the details and events of your life, extracting the wisdom you have gained from your experience.

This "quintessential state" is not just for yourself alone: all that you have gained from life ultimately contributes to the evolutionary process of the Universe. Thus nothing is ever lost, nothing is ever meaningless: it is all part of the conscious, spiritual, evolutionary process of the Universe.

Now we have arrived at a significant transitional state of consciousness, corresponding to the plane or perspective of consciousness called *Jabarut*.

As Ibn 'Arabi says of this level, "At an advanced stage God reveals Himself without using these clues, these *ayat*," or signs. Thus it is a stage of direct revelation of the Divine Being—a pure disclosure of the Divine meaningfulness that does not rest upon clues.

Suddenly, everything makes sense; the kind of sense that differs from the way we typically think in our everyday minds. This state is implicit in the word *Jabar* itself, which means "the bone-setter," or the chiropractor who aligns your bones correctly. On a spiritual level this means that you have been through a process where your thinking has been broken apart, then set right. It predominates over your ordinary way of thinking. Like the chaos theories in physics, it is that rare condition when order emerges out of chaos, and everything suddenly falls into place.

Nowhere is this more evident than in everyday life, where it seems as if so much is askew, in chaos and disorder. Very often you find the wrong person in the right place and the right person in the wrong place. People act unreasonably, and events go wrong to the point of disaster. Yet somehow, over the course of evolution, disparate, random events find their correspondence with each other, and things begin to fall into place. The right person, for instance, ends up in the right place. Perhaps they thought they were in the right place, but if a person is really in the wrong place, they can't hold out very long. Something always happens, and they're forced to resign or move. So ultimately, life is a process of getting things right—but it takes till the ends of time to make things right. The two l's of the word *Allah* represent the two throws of an arrow that are related in the story of the Prophet Muhammad and the *miraj*. According to that story, Muhammad was transported from the Ka'abah in Mecca to Celestial Jerusalem—a heavenly place which is not of the physical world. But, as it is told, he only got within "two throws" (*kab*, in Arabic) of an arrow. Like that tense moment when a marksman's bow is drawn, when all that remains between his aim of hitting the target is the short distance between his hand and the bow, this stage signifies getting very, very close to something. So at this point in your journey, you are very near to the Celestial Jerusalem—or a big breakthrough in meditation.

This whole process that I am describing thus far in the *dhikr* is embodied in the story of St. John of the Cross, in which he went through the dark night of the soul, questioning all that he thought to be true, then suddenly, out of the void of nothingness, meaningfulness was revealed to him, which he could not have grasped through his understanding.

Then, after *Jabarut*, you reach the level of *Lahut*, which signifies the Divine programming. Here we find the intention which is in view in the structuring of the pieces of the puzzle which one could not see when they were randomly scattered in the state of chaos. So it's really seeing that things have to be how they are—something that's very difficult to perceive with our ordinary understanding. It takes this level of consciousness to finally see life through the eyes of God— to see the programming behind the Universe. That's *Lahut*.

In Islam, *Lahut* is also called the Divine Treasury.

As the Qur'an says, "Everything has its likeness in the Divine Treasury." The ancient Sufi Niffari said, "I cannot give you the secret of the Divine Treasury." As we explored before in the chapter on the Divine Qualities, there is a level of consciousness where the archetypes exist in their pure form. These archetypes are reflected in the less-than-perfect realm of creation; Ibn 'Arabi says that the angels build a ladder between these two realms. In other words, behind our earthly inheritance that has come down to us in an imperfect form through our ancestry, and that has become further limited through our own flaws and failings, lies a realm of perfect archetypes. This is the level of consciousness that we aspire to when we repeat the different names of God—trying to reach beyond our narrow representation of qualities in order to connect to the Divine Qualities in their perfect archetypal form.

Now, having journeyed through the various planes of consciousness, you reach the plane of *Hahut*, which one experiences when intoning and thinking of the "h" of *'llah*. At this level one grasps the oneness behind multiplicity, the state the yogis call *samadhi*. At this pinnacle one grasps the Being of God, rather than the intention. One's identity becomes immersed in the Oneness. This is awakening beyond life; no words can truly describe this state of consciousness—they can only point to it. I can only attempt to convey it through describing a retreat I once took in Jerusalem in the Cave of the Ascension at the top of the Mount of Olives, from which, according to some accounts, Jesus ascended into heaven. The access to that cave is through a mosque. You enter by going down a set of steps; inside there is a little skylight, and recesses in the wall. There is a foot-mark in the rock that is said to be the mark made by Christ's foot as he was on his way to heaven. At the time I was on my retreat, I was continuously repeating the *dhikr*. Imagine how you would feel doing the *dhikr* in this holy cave, certainly frequented by Jesus, and where most probably Melchizedek lived while the tribes were living in tents.

At this stage of the *dhikr*, you could think of yourself as a pendulum that is moving in space; the top of this pendulum represents the eternal, unchanging, and immortal aspect. Suspended in this state of eternity, you awaken beyond life; you perceive the physical world—your memory, your personality—but dimly, as if it had fallen out of focus. All that remains is a quintessence of your being. You find yourself distanced from the world, as though you have been able to lift yourself beyond existence. In this state you are completely freed from the limitations of your narrow perspectives. You've found the freedom that you longed for. It is what Buddha referred to as being "outside the wheel." As he said at the end of his retreat under the Bodhi tree, "It is the freedom from determinism, from causality."

But the *dhikr* does not culminate here; rather, on the syllable *hu*. For the more free one is internally, the more one can enter into life to help people find the freedom they are yearning for. Thus in the *dhikr*, awakening beyond life is always followed by awakening in life.

For example, I was not allowed to stay in the Cave of the Ascension all night—it was a very strange thing to come out of that state and see everyone caught up in their worries, anxieties, and preoccupations. But in the state I was in, I still could see the unity underlying all existence.

The organ of the physical heart is the instrument that helps you to awaken in life, while keeping the perspective you gained when you awakened beyond life. For reconnecting to the world after a retreat does not have to take away your awareness of what is behind it all. Instead, where before you were at a loss to make sense of things, now you can see the Divine Intention at work, including the Divine investiture of freedom to each fragment of Himself. This is bringing the celestial sphere to the realm of everyday existence; it is awakening heaven on earth. In other words, all is God. This is a wholly different way of thinking about God than as "up there." Rather, the whole practice of the *dhikr* is to make God present.

I remember events from my own life when I have felt such moments. During the seventies, for instance, there were various Eastern teachers of different movements who were inspiring large numbers of people. One day, we were all invited to the Monastery of the Sacred Heart in Ohio. At one point in this gathering, all the teachers came together to celebrate their worship together. It was incredible—all these spiritual leaders who normally never would have met before, and who sometimes criticized each other's teachings, joined in what I would call a cosmic celebration. It was my life's dream; something that I had always longed for. Something was coming through at that moment in time; it was as if for one brief moment, we had opened the doors between the physical world and the celestial spheres. What came through in our acts of glorification was a reminiscence of the celestial spheres and of that original state of innocence that we can still find in the child within. Thus, in conclusion, one could say that the practice of the *dhikr* incorporates within it the whole mystery of the Divine Being manifesting in both the transcendent and immanent dimensions.

SEVEN

HEAVEN ON EARTH:

AWAKENING CONSCIENCE
IN EVERYDAY LIFE

"The purpose of life is the knowledge that God gains of His perfection in our imperfection."

— HAZRAT INAYAT KHAN

"Where are you to find God if not in the God-conscious?"

— HAZRAT INAYAT KHAN

◆

As this book comes to a close, and we prepare to return to the world, it is my hope that we will re-enter with a difference, carrying with us something of the atmosphere, attunement, and vibration of the Divine mystery that we have experienced on our journey across the landscapes of altered consciousness. Just like those

astronauts who returned from their sojourn profoundly
altered by their dazzling view of earth from outer space,
so, too, can the transcendent experience catalyze a similar transformation in how we look at life. Though the
mystical encounter goes deeper than words can convey,
tangible traces of it can be seen in the actions we take,
the values we uphold, and the ideals we strive for. In
effect, what I am trying to say is that the illumination
of consciousness leads inevitably to the awakening of
conscience. This enables us to fulfill the purpose of our
lives and actualize the unfurling of the potentialities of
our beings.

But the awakening of conscience—our responsive-
ness to the needs of the world—is not an easy path.
Mystics, especially, are often torn between the strong
desire to lose themselves in the totality and blissful
oneness of God and the unique responsibilities each
person has been given to fulfill in this life. For example, there is the natural responsibility we each bear
toward the personal kingdom of family, friends, and co-
workers. But how far does our responsibility extend?
Does it go beyond our immediate circle? Is the starv-
ing, homeless person we pass on the street also a part of
our responsibility?

To answer that question, I would say that there is
no limit to the responsibility we bear toward others.
For example, at every moment someone is being tortured for political reasons in a concentration camp or
prison. Isn't that our responsibility? Couldn't we join
Amnesty International and write letters or make phone

calls to try to make a difference in the lives of those victims of repression who are being tortured and stripped
of their basic human rights? When you look at life from
this perspective, it seems counterproductive to allow
ourselves to be totally lost in God. In the state of
samadhi, for instance, there is little emphasis on taking
responsibility for the world. In Sufism, however,
the emphasis is on becoming a vice-regent of God
who is accountable for healing the human condition.
Thus an overemphasis on *samadhi* will lead to otherworldliness, whereas the Sufi orientation will lead a
person to become more effective in life.

Indeed, whereas the way of the ascetic is to give up
the world, the way of the Sufi is to build a beautiful
world of beautiful people. Instead of thinking that such
an endeavor conflicts with the spiritual ideal of detachment, it is a goal that, to Sufis, represents the fulfillment of the Divine Purpose on earth—an expression of
the Divine impulse that is called *Ishq Allah*, or the love
of God for creation. Our endeavor to build a beautiful
world of beautiful people is the way we actualize the
Divine *Ishq Allah*. The manifestation of Divine Love,
Ishq Allah, is the longing to bring heaven on earth and
to make our dreams come true. The deeply felt nostalgia to experience heaven on earth is a basic drive behind
all of our lives. It is reflected in our yearning to be able
to find the freedom to pursue the destiny for which we
were born. It is through living out our purpose in day-
to-day life that we actuate the archetypes hidden
within the Divine Treasury. In short, creating heaven

on earth is the responsibility each one of us bears to make God a reality.

On this subject Hazrat Inayat Khan is very clear, stating that the way of the Sufi is not the way of the ascetic, and that everything that has been gained in life is the result of enthusiasm. As he says, "The power that you gain by pursuing your interest will give you the ability to take upon yourself a greater challenge than you have taken on so far. We gain in power by pursuing our purpose in life." Thus for Hazrat Inayat Khan, how we handle situations and what we strive to accomplish in life are extremely important parts of spiritual development. But he cautions that our personal motivations do limit our power. For if our motivation is only for personal gain or personal power, it narrows the scope of our achievement. Ultimately, the motivation underlying our pursuits should not be wholly personal, but a desire to be of service. The ideal of the Sufi is to become involved in life, and yet, at the same time, in the depths of our being, to be independent of external circumstances. As Hazrat Inayat Khan says, we are each tested in life to the degree to which we are free.

What does it mean to live a life that is simultaneously both involved and detached? To love people unconditionally with all one's heart and yet endure their constant pinpricks and woundings valiantly? The integral relationship between involvement and detachment is symbolized by the Sufi symbol: a heart that is subjected to the gravity pull from earth at the top and the bottom, with two wings providing the redeeming uplift of detachment and independence that, says Hazrat Inayat Khan, "enable the soul to fly." In other words, if we raise our consciousness into the solitude of oneness we are very alone, unless our indifference is balanced with love. And while attachment and dependence upon people and things are the commonplace condition if we are to fulfill our purpose in life, the ideal is to be able to fulfill that purpose while at the same time maintaining our freedom of spirit. Then, despite the worst suffering and tribulation, our consciousness will still be able to touch upon states of sublime exaltation—and that is the only way to bring the glory of the heavens into the earth plane. As previously quoted in this book, it is the message implicit in Shams of Tabriz's statement that the dervish is "a palace in a ruin." The ultimate value of our being is present even within its defilement, even by the worst conditions; thus the "palace in a ruin" symbolizes the triumph of that which is of lasting and eternal value over the powers of destruction.

Muhasaba: The process of differentiating between what is of ultimate value and that which is transient and fleeting is embodied in the Sufi practice of *Muhasaba,* or the examination of conscience. While it is a process that is used at the beginning of a retreat, as explored previously, it is also useful for seekers to re-examine their values and ideals at the end of a retreat as, often, genuine spiritual transformation can spark a revolution in one's priorities. Hazrat Inayat Khan,

for instance, speaks about how the awakening of consciousness brings about a shift in values away from
what most people pursue to what really matters. For
when we awaken to the glory of the heavens, he says, it
is as if those things that once mattered so much suddenly don't matter anymore; the things that perturb
people don't perturb us very much anymore; the things
that once had value now seem to have no value what-
soever.

This shift in values is the foundation of the practice
of *Muhasaba*; it is not about working with consciousness, but with conscience—the art of differentiating
between what is of lasting, authentic value and what is
of a more transient, fleeting nature. Indeed, the way to
raise our consciousness above the constraints of ordinary life is to place a higher priority on those things
which we consider to be of greater value. From a spiritual perspective, this is like dropping the ballast that
keeps us prisoner on the earth plane, and enabling our
soul to rise. Over the course of our lives many of us lose
sight of those values that we had when we were
younger—those idyllic ideals we entertained in our
naïve youth. Perhaps it's not true of everyone, but I was
taught that God is beautiful, and that you are supposed
to aspire toward something noble in your life. Yet
somehow, these drives get waylaid by the demands of
life. It starts very early; slowly, at school, we begin to
doubt and mistrust our higher aspirations.

Thus, when you begin the process of examining
your conscience, it is helpful to weigh your everyday

actions against those ideals you once held to be important and see whether they are still important for you.
Now ask yourself what you are doing to live up to your
ideals. You cannot really begin to live up to them until
you know what they are. For this reason it helps to
begin the practice of *Muhasaba* by asking yourself a
series of questions designed to highlight your true priorities in life, such as, "What are the values for which
I stand?" or, "What are the motivations behind the
decisions I make and the way that I handle my problems?" and, "What are the things in life that I value
over others? What is it that I want to achieve with my
life?" Such questions help to clarify the individual
identity and purpose in life, which often evolves out of
our strong personal likes and dislikes. What we truly
value, for example, often becomes clear when a particular pursuit or ideal pushes an inner button of recognition, so to speak, prompting the response, "This is
me."

To help in this process, you could make a catalogue
of your values. For one person, music might possess a
tremendous value, while for another dedication and
being of service is what matters most. Someone else
may hold the need to offer compassion to people who
are suffering as ultimate value. The wish to create
beauty and to eliminate grossness is also one of
humankind's essential goals—not just visual beauty
but the kind of beauty that results from right actions.
Another may have the desire to build a beautiful world
amid an ugly, degenerate environment. Still others

might value the quality of majesty—the ability of certain noble people to manifest a very high standard in their lives. Or, to a few, what seems most important may be the ideal of restoring sacredness to a desacralized world. Many discover through the process of *Muhasaba* that they are motivated by a powerful need to discover the meaningfulness of life. It is only then that one can justify one's claims to try to awaken humanity to the rapture of the mystery of existence.

Indeed, when awakening the Divine Conscience within oneself, it is helpful to submit the values that we hold to the test of what they ultimately might mean to humanity. The physicist David Bohm, for instance, has said that in the future, creativity will be meaningful only if it is relevant to all humanity. Thus there are four categories that I feel reflect the ultimate values of the spirituality of the future: achievement in service; the creative unfurling of our potentialities; the realization of the meaningfulness of life; and awakening to the transfiguring effect of the sacred upon one's being.

The process of articulating and proclaiming the values that we stand for leads inevitably to the question of whether or not our lives match our ideals, or whether we just pay them lip service. We tend to find excuses for not honoring our ideals. "Circumstances don't allow me to pursue that ideal," we say to ourselves, or, "That ideal is just not compelling enough for me to make sacrifices for." One dilemma I've often witnessed among people trying to live up to their ideals is that on the one hand they wish to be involved in life, work, and relationships. Yet at the same time those involvements limit their ability to fulfill their life's expectations. A person struggling with this problem needs to see very clearly if such a constraint is circumstantial, and therefore can be changed, or if the limitation is really in his emotions or way of thinking. We can't always be free from circumstances, but we can always attempt to find freedom in ourselves.

The only way to be sure that we are doing everything we can to promote our values in real-life situations is to ask ourselves, "What am I prepared to do to pursue that value?" If we are not prepared to do whatever is necessary, it's not a real value—it's an abstract ideal. In order to answer this question as truthfully as possible, we must be very, very honest with ourselves. We must learn to differentiate among our personal needs, our underlying motivations, and our ideals. To what extent, for instance, are we prepared to sacrifice a personal need in order to support a value? Perhaps we delight in doing something, say, boating, or playing tennis. At the same time we also value something more, such as fighting for the rights of prisoners of conscience. If it came down to a choice, would we really opt for the things we value the most? That is, would we sacrifice the things we value less? If we are not prepared to do this, then that value remains fictitious.

This kind of moral authenticity is what Hazrat Inayat Khan meant when he said to "shatter your ideal on the rock of truth." We can formulate all kinds of ideals, but they will never become real motivations in our lives unless we are prepared to make the sacrifice that is required to pursue them. However, it is also important that this practice be done without harsh self-judgment, and with a degree of balance. For if we excessively deny ourselves our personal wishes, then we will feel sorry for ourselves—and then we will not have the joy we need in order to pursue our higher ideals. This is an individual matter of conscience that is different for each person. We can ascertain this balance by observing ourselves as though we were another person—objectively, without personal bias, justification, or self-criticism—and by asking ourselves the simplest of questions: "Why am I doing what I am doing?" This way we can determine for ourselves the balance between those ideals that we really wish to pursue, and those personal needs that will keep us from falling into self-pity.

This moral process can be extended to our relationships with other people as well. We might ask ourselves, for instance, what our motivations are with regard to our friendships or intimate ties. Are we involved with them in order to gain some advantage for our own well-being, or is it out of consideration for the well-being of the other person? Is there any manipulation going on? Are we being totally honest? These kinds of questions can even be included in our dialogues with others, exploring the nature of the expectations of our relationships, or expressing disappointment because these expectations have not been met. Unfortunately, it's all too often true that we involve ourselves in life because we want to get something out of it for ourselves. Thus a certain amount of concupiscence in our behavior curtails the unfurling of our being. But we can never become the beautiful beings that we are meant to become if we are motivated solely by our own advancement at the cost of others.

The culmination of the process of *Muhasaba* is to see how our noblest impulses are an expression of the Divine impulse toward manifestation. We can become conscious of this impulse that is moving us toward the fulfillment of our life's purpose by thinking of a funnel—the large end representing the Divine, and the small end our individual ego. The more conscious we become of the moral quandaries and decision-making processes—or all that is in between the large and the small, or the Divine and the human dimensions—the closer we come to awakening the Divine conscience within us. For there is no doubt that pursuing our ideal gives us spiritual power. In fact, it makes us into heroes. Pursuing our personal objective can also give us power, but the danger is that power corrupts, encouraging in the person a despotic attitude and a capability for ruthlessly manipulating people—as we see so often in the history of the world. But that's not real power. This kind of inauthentic power will collapse when confronted with truth, like the Nazi war criminals who, when put before the commission of investigation, began to collapse. The reverse of this is the example of Christ, who did not relent when faced with the power of Rome.

In this regard, I think of a wonderful man I met many years ago. He came to my seminars in Germany after the war. He lived just like a hermit, in a simple room. Yet he employed 5,000 people, providing for their health and dental benefits. Though he bore enormous responsibility for others, he didn't want anything for himself. He wanted only to be of service. He was a wonderful man. He wasn't a hermit, because he was right there in the middle of life. But he was a living example of bringing spirituality into everyday life. I tell this story because people are not only looking for guidance, they are looking for support to put their ideals into action. Once we have had a realization that there are more important things in life than social prestige or material wealth, then we need faith to implement our visions and ideals. Hazrat Inayat Khan describes this as swimming with a person who is floundering in the water. Not only do we have to keep ourselves afloat, but we have to keep afloat that person who is unable to save himself. That's where our faith is drawn upon by people of little faith. If we start doubting our own spiritual ideals, however, we cause the person who is looking to us for support to sink in the water and drown.

In addition, we have to have faith that life will become better. Some people, for instance, are able to think of their flaws and failures as a springboard to creativity. Winston Churchill was a stutterer, for instance, and he became one of the greatest orators of our time. Stephen Hawking can communicate only through a high-tech computer, and yet he is a brilliant physicist. In this way, we can consider the circumstances of our lives as a catalyst which enlists our creativity. If we simply deplore the circumstances in which we find ourselves, then we have lost precious opportunities. As Hazrat Inayat Khan puts it, this "passion for the unattainable"—the timeless quest of pursuing an ideal in order to make it a reality—is what makes great beings.

JOAN OF ARC
AND NOOR INAYAT KHAN
∞

Now, I would like to introduce the stories of two women, one ancient and one modern, whose lives were the living embodiment of their ideals. I will begin first with the story of Joan of Arc. Even as a young girl of thirteen, she heard voices speaking to her in the ringing of the church bells. Then, at the age of fifteen, she had become certain that she was to go on a mission to restore the king of France to his throne. At that time, the British had besieged many of the cities of France, and the Dauphin, the deposed French king, was a weak character. But then along came this amazing young girl, following her voices; not only that—she dressed in men's clothes. Somehow, through the strength of her conviction, she managed to persuade the governor of the city to let her visit the Dauphin.

At that time the Dauphin was living in a castle.

After a long adventure, during which Joan of Arc collected an army of volunteers who were impressed by her mission and her power, she was able not only to have an audience with the Dauphin but to convince him to follow her. Together, they rode their horses through the countryside, conquering most of the British forces. Finally they took Orleans, which was a very strong garrison—a great feat. After they conquered Orleans, they went to the cathedral of Rheims, where the kings of France were crowned. There, the Dauphin, who was under the protection of this little maid who had the strength of the conviction of her voices, and who was just seventeen years old, was crowned king.

Then, on her way to Rouen, Joan of Arc was captured, dragged off her horse, thrown into jail, and placed in chains. She was put on trial and subjected to an inquisition by all the learned Church Fathers. Despite her proclamations that she was following her voices, she was tortured and then dragged out of the cell where she was compelled to sign a special document in which she dismissed her voices as nothing more than an illusion or hallucination. A few days later, however, she recanted, realizing that her voices were true and that she could not go against them. For this act Joan of Arc was subjected to more torture, and then burned alive at the stake.

This is one more story of the brutality of the powers that be, the ego power of the people condemning her, and the fanaticism of the theologians. Joan of Arc was a frail girl who didn't know how to read or write, much less argue; she couldn't begin to protect herself. Her brief relapse was a natural result of doubting herself in the face of those she thought were scholars and authorities. But it was only two days before she recanted the confession wrested from her against her will. For this, she was eventually burned at the stake as a witch who had dangerous, magical powers. She was also excommunicated from the Church. The irony of this story is that even today if someone hears voices, they are drugged, or locked up in an asylum. Just a few centuries later, however, the Catholic Church itself recanted and took back its decision to condemn her. The story of Joan of Arc stands for the valor of the many women in the world whose courage has been repressed through the ages. Behind Joan of Arc's story is something that we are coming to honor in our time—the value of the Divine Feminine.

In this regard, I think of my sister, Noor, who was such a gentle, gifted, and idealistic person. She played the harp and wrote children's books and was planning to start a magazine for teenagers called *New Age*. And like Joan of Arc, she, too, experienced the horror of unbearable cruelty, but on the part of the Nazis. Her story begins when, during World War II, she heard about the tortures inflicted upon the Jews by the Nazis, and responded by volunteering as a radio telegrapher. She was eventually recruited by the BSC (British Security Coordination) and sent to Paris as a secret agent to maintain radio contact between the War Office and the underground forces of resistance—

one of the most dangerous missions in occupied
Europe. Working under the assumed code name
"Madeleine," she transmitted messages between the
British War Office and the French Resistance, which
were crucial in the success of the landing in Normandy.
Almost immediately upon her arrival, however, a large
part of the leaders of the French secret network she
belonged to were rounded up and arrested—leaving
Noor as the sole transmitter. Though her superiors in
London ordered her to leave, offering to send a plane
to pick her up, she refused. She knew that without her
all communications would be cut off. Placing herself
in the most grave danger, Noor continued transmit-
ting from July through October, when she was
betrayed to the Gestapo, who had thus found her codes
and messages. Taken to their headquarters in the
Avenue Foch, Noor was imprisoned and subjected to
intense, grueling interrogations.

I was at the trial afterward. There, I heard the details
of the capture: how the Nazi who arrested Noor had
received a telephone call from a Frenchwoman who said
she had the address of my sister and wanted to sell it
for 100,000 francs. The Nazi met her on a bench near
the Parc Monceau in Paris, and the transaction was
made. The consequence of this betrayal was that the
brother of this very woman, as well as hundreds of other
people, were arrested and tortured. I saw that woman
at the trial. She was acquitted by the judge because the
lawyer said, "We've suffered enough through the

Nazis, and now it is a Nazi who is the only witness here against our French people."

After her arrest, Noor made an attempt to escape from the Gestapo Headquarters in Paris, but was caught, then thrown in a lorry and taken to a prison in Karlsruhe. There, she was handcuffed and chained, and kept in total isolation for ten months. Then she was transferred to the Dachau concentration camp. The *gauleiter* (Nazi guard) kept on kicking her with his heavy boots as she lay on a cement floor in chains, suffering agony from enormous hematomas all over her body. She was in agony throughout the night, exposed on the cement floor, without shelter. The next day she was whipped and hit to the point that she was, as a witness said, a bloody mess. Then she was made to kneel and was shot in the head from behind. But she didn't cry. Her last words were *"Vive la liberté."* Apparently there was still some motion in her body when she was thrown into the oven that is still in Dachau.

BECOMING A
KNIGHT OF LIGHT
∽

Indeed, amid the cruelty, ignorance, vanity, greed, grossness, and the overwhelming despair of human beings exists a "rescue operation" of those whose aim is to share their compassion with those who suffer. This

is the ultimate expression of the awakening of conscience. I am not talking about only the awakening of
the mind, but also the awakening of the emotion of the
heart to the power of unconditional love that material-
ized this physical Universe into being.

Confronted with the depths of the suffering of all
beings, the person who is truly awakened cannot help
but be motivated by Divine Love to become a kind of
"knight of awakening," whose code of chivalry is that
of the highest dedication to service. For the initiate who
has arrived at this realization, withdrawing from life in
order to obtain enlightenment for oneself is the
supreme egotism. One tends to withdraw into one's
personal "I" when suffering. However, often the con-
trry is true. For instance, I once spoke with a Frenchwoman who had been in the Resistance with my sister,
Noor. She told me that she had been tortured to such a
point that she became blind, and was thrown into a cell
as dead. Yet, she recounted to me, even then, she continued to smile. The reason? Because, she explained,
"The Nazis enjoyed listening to us scream—therefore,
we decided not to scream. But when the pain became
unbearable, our spirits left our bodies, as in out-of-body
projection. From that heightened vantage point, we
were able to ignore our oppressors, realizing that while
they could inflict torture on our bodies, they had no
power over our souls." In yet another case, I recall meet-
ing a man who had been tortured by both the Nazis and
the Russians. Unbelievably, he said he had been able to

forgive his tormentors by attuning to the consciousness of Christ—thus forgiving them as Christ had forgiven His torturers.

Can you imagine taking a vow to become a knight of light as part of your spiritual practice? The work would entail protecting the victims of manipulation and greed; in addition, you would act to counter the actions of those who cause suffering to others. Assuming a role in a cosmic knighthood of service, however, requires attuning to the spiritual power that flows all the way down through the hierarchy of beings who form the spiritual government of the world to those on the earth plane working to better the human condition. For when people act in the name of the governance of the Universe rather than out of their own personal incentive, they are empowered—the power that creates miracles, brings dreams into reality, and establishes heaven on earth. But this cannot happen without those who have dedicated and consecrated themselves to act as emissaries of the governance of the One and Only Being, God.

The only weapons that are permissible in this cosmic crusade are lances of light that dispel the darkness. In fact, the fulfillment of such a task requires of us that we awaken the light even in our own bodies. It also means discovering the light in others as well, reinforcing each others' luminosity in mutual recognition.

As I mentioned before, the path of the Sufi initiate is the path of light. If you are among those who seek light in their lives, whatever its origin, you've knocked on the right door. It requires a commitment that the Zoroastrian Magi used to make: to fight for the victory of light over darkness. This vow has many expressions: one is "Let there be light." Ultimately, light is the emergence of truth that has been hidden by a cover-up of manipulation and dishonesty in life. It is my hope that the ranks of the selfless, who bring light wherever they go, will increase beyond measure, as that is the cure for the world's ills.

THE REALIZATION OF THE HEART: HOW EMOTIONS CULTIVATE IDEALISM

∞

When we talk about the awakening of conscience, we are also talking about the awakening of the emotions. Sufis, as I have said, make a distinction between the realization of the heart and the realization of the mind. Some people suffer, for instance, as they grow older and lose faith in those ideals that they once held high. One is exposed to doubt at a young age when one finds disappointment, encounters disenchantment, and fears that one's dreams were merely unfounded Utopian fantasies—thus losing one's trust in the marvel of life. It was for this very reason that during the late sixties and early seventies I began organizing meditation camps for young people—I wanted to urge young people to keep their spirits up,

Heaven on Earth

whatever the circumstances. The drama of life is always
woven through with emotions of despair or anger against
the incongruity and unfairness of circumstances, as well
as exhaustion from the never-ending quest just to survive. As a result of this stress, the emotions dry up and
the heart burns out, extinguishing the flame of our values and ideals. Thus the important question becomes
how to feel once again; how to resonate both with the
suffering and the joy of the human condition without
being so overwhelmed by the enormity of the world's
problems that we lose hope.

The great classical composers give us a wordless
example of what I mean by the "realization of the heart."
Beethoven, for instance, was courageous enough to
believe that society can be improved; behind that fragile
and powerful soul pummeled by the tragedy of his deaf-
ness was a being of tremendous, heroic self-confidence.
Brahms, as well, transformed terrible psychological suffering into joy, not just at the soul level, but right in the
human heart. Handel brought us the sacredness, the
sense of glory, that one discovers in one's act of glorification. If you enter into the thinking of these composers,
you can feel what I mean by the difference between awakening in life and awakening beyond life.

As a meditation practice, cultivate the realization of
the heart by first becoming conscious of the many different levels of emotion. Buddha described different
levels of emotion. It is like awakening a high sensitivity of the heart. The task is to watch not only your emotions but also the effects of the emotions of others on us

and ours on others. The spectrum of emotion ranges from the extreme, vulgar emotions of violence and lust to anger, jealousy, and resentment, to more ordinary emotions such as the desire for recognition, empowerment, status, and possessions. At the far end of this spectrum are the rare emotions of sacredness experienced during worship or during moments of prayer or meditation. This is the emotion of the soul.

The word that captures the emotion of the soul is exaltation. It may begin as admiration: admiring music, architecture, poetry, art, intelligence, or beauty. In addition, there is also an emotion that comes from awe at the miracle of life—the pulse of life beating right there on your street and in your neighborhood. Compared to the more low-key emotional attunement of people, this is like cultivating a taste for the sublime. So, as you can see, emotions are the seedbed of values. Thus part of the task of awakening conscience is to sensitize one's heart to the more sublime and exalted values of the soul and spirit. Our hearts become so bruised and hardened that we begin to lose the capacity to feel the higher ranges of the spectrum of emotion. Cultivating these emotional values, rather than killing them with cyncism and mistrust, leads us into a transfigured world that lies just behind the physical world. This leads to a perspective that attunes our feelings to the emotions of that world—the emotions of the soul.

The doorway to experiencing the emotion of the soul is through the child within us—for it is the pure heart that leads the way to a higher attunement of consciousness. The secret to entering the consciousness of the child within is to remember the state we were in before our birth; this will kindle heavenly emotions within us. Returning to the state of the child means to become stripped of all guile, manipulation, intrigue, and deception.

I once had the opportunity to watch and listen to the choreography of what Leonard Bernstein called *The Mass,* while having been warned never to go there because it is a horrible travesty of sacredness. It began with a Greek bass singer who was singing the part of a great priest. When the priest would say, "Let us pray," everybody in the congregation knelt in devotion before a glorious altar. The priest was so revered that people brought him gifts; in turn, he gave them a blessing. *The Mass* built up to a wonderful peak; the rapport between the priest and his congregants was superb.

Then, just at this high point, a skeptic entered the scene, a clever, witty man, who said, "This is all just a show." Though the people were a bit put off, the priest still kept their attention. Then another skeptic came on the scene who was even more powerful than the last, saying, in effect, "Do you see that altar? Do you think it's holy? It's just wood and candles. Why do you think it's holy? It's all in your mind." Then doubt really began to corrode the hearts of the people. Still, the great priest managed to enjoin people to stay; somehow he had power over them.

Soon, however, doubt began to gain the upper hand. Lay priests began divesting themselves. Even the great priest went behind the altar and removed his vestments. Then he broke the altar and threw the candles in fury. Everyone collapsed into despair, and there was total darkness. Then, out of that darkness emerged a boy about twelve years old who was holding a candle and singing a beautiful chant. People began to stand up again, for they sensed that this was the real thing. To me, that moment during *The Mass* seemed as if the people of doubt on the earth were listening to the language of the heavens speaking to them through a child. This is the voice that we must listen to; we've become so jaded and sophisticated that we've lost the sacredness of our being. Thus it is critical that we place more value on those rare moments when we feel inspired or uplifted. It is during such moments that something of the heavens comes through. This does not mean that we must renounce the wisdom we have gained as we grow older; in fact, the great skill of life is to be able to maintain the innocence of a child in one's heart while at the same time possessing mastery and control. The combination of these two modes of being is a great art.

Achieving such a synthesis of qualities is an ongoing, lifelong process. None of us is immune from being hurt in life; every day, we hand our heart over to people who challenge us, saying, in effect, "Are you still so naïve as to believe in a spiritual reality?" or again, "If you don't do what I want you to, I'll break your heart." If we make a gift of ourselves out of love, we become vulnerable. Yet, somehow, just like the child who continues to trust no matter how many times he is rejected or rebuffed, the goal is to go on trusting in life itself. The miracle is that then a foundation of trust begins to build up; as people value the trust we give to them, they begin to feel safe with us. When we have attained this spiritual realization of the heart, then we will have developed a heart-power that reaches right into the souls of people. For, as I have experienced myself, it is our suffering, our broken heart, that gives us insight into the suffering of others. Not pity but sharing in the suffering ourselves because we, too, have known sorrow and loss. The extraordinary thing is that the insight of the heart is the magic that unleashes talents and potentialities within people that have been blocked as a result of their suffering.

Finally, it is the realization and knowledge of the heart that will enable us to reconcile the irreconcilables of our life: to honor our sadness, while at the same time experiencing joy. Many times throughout my life I have had a vision of a dervish who is dancing on thorns with a crown of thorns on his head, and yet who is in a state of ecstasy. Through this vision, I understood that despite the darkness of the moment when He hung dying on the cross, alone and abandoned, Christ was in a state of supreme beatitude—a state of consciousness which could never have been attained if things had occurred the way people thought they should have. Indeed, behind the Crucifixion of Christ on earth, a jubilant coronation in the heavens was taking place. In the same way, a resurrection is taking place behind the crucifixion of our own suffering—the joy of being released from the limitations of our human condition.

And now, I will close with several mottos that have formed a perennial refrain in my teachings and that I have referred to frequently throughout this book. One is from my father, Hazrat Inayat Khan, who said to remember that a defeat can aver itself to be a victory, and that a victory can aver itself to be a defeat. So, what I would say to you is this: Don't judge yourself by how externally successful you have been. In the same way, don't denigrate yourself if you have not lived up to your expectations—furthermore, you cannot expect justice in the world nor can you always achieve the position that is rightfully due you. In this regard, the opinions of others are relative—so be careful not to make your self-esteem dependent upon the opinions of others.

An even deeper motto is the phrase of the Sufi Shams of Tabriz, who said, "The man of God is a palace in a ruin." This means that the heart broken by life is subjected to the inroads of the malignant beings. The old violins and cellos of the eighteenth century, however, are a wonderful exemplification for the Divine music that comes from the broken heart. More than two centuries old, these instruments have fissures and breaks—and yet they sound much better than new ones. There is a French phrase for this condition that translates, "They have a wound in their soul." The reason why clarinets and oboes have different tones is because they have flaws. If they were perfect, they could not contribute their sound together with that of other instruments to the richness of the orchestra.

So if you think that you are handicapped in some way, you will find that your compensation for it is a quality that you wouldn't have cultivated if it were not for that innate flaw. Indeed, one is never so strong as when one is broken. When you grasp that mystery, then you will be able to see how what seemed like a loss or a defeat is instead a victory, and that how you are broken is where you are whole. That was the message of Christ. I have tried, in all my teachings, to bring forth a message of light. I sincerely hope that it will help you in some way. Especially if you are going through a dark night of the soul, remember that it is because you are not aware of your own light—and it is light that will show you the way. And while I hope that some of the skills and meditations that I have presented will be helpful to you, they are useful only as a ladder in attaining the essential objective—awakening consciousness and conscience in everyday life.

For more information contact:

Sufi Order International

P. O. Box 30065

Seattle, WA 98103

(206) 525–6992

SufiOrder@compuserve.com

www.sufiorder.org